Her Majesty Queen Elizabeth II
Patron
The Soldiers' and Airmen's Scripture Readers Association

Sovereign Service

The Story of SASRA 1838–2013

Brigadier Ian Dobbie OBE

The Soldiers' and Airmen's
Scripture Readers Association

First published 1988
Revised edition 2013

The Soldiers' and Airmen's
Scripture Readers Association
Havelock House, Barrack Road
Aldershot, Hants. GU11 3NP

ISBN 0 9512486 0 X

CONTENTS

FOREWORD to First Edition

By

John Pollock

That Christian hero of Victorian England, Major General Sir Henry Havelock, would have been pleased with the story described in this excellent book. I well remember unfolding Havelock's wafer-thin letters from India (rescued in the nick of time from mice in a cellar) in which he described his pioneer work for the social and spiritual welfare of his men.

Havelock was not the actual founder of The Soldiers' and Airmen's Scripture Readers Association, but his example inspired them. As Colonel Dobbie shows, SASRA is the union of two organisations. The earlier began in 1838, and therefore 1988 is the right date for a 150th Anniversary celebration.

Ian Dobbie, grandson of the fine Christian soldier who became world famous for his defence of Malta in the Second World War, brings the SASRA story alive. He blends contemporary accounts of earlier days, deftly updating antique language without destroying atmosphere; and he gives much information about the sterling work of the Scripture Readers in the Army and Royal Air Force today.

I am very honoured to have been asked to write a Foreword, perhaps because two of my biographies are of men who played important parts in SASRA's origins – General Havelock and D L Moody.

I also have warm memories of Scripture Readers from my war-service in the Coldstream Guards. Most of the Readers were older men as the younger had been recalled to the Colours. Some were a little quaint but they were very loyal to Christ and His Gospel, and to the traditions of the service. They worked closely with the Chaplains. The Scripture Readers, because they were not officers (most were ex-sergeants) could move more easily in the barrack rooms, and many a young guardsman was helped by the right word at the right time.

I also have vivid memories of the late Lieutenant General Sir Arthur Smith, for many years Chairman of SASRA. I am very glad that Colonel Dobbie reprints the obituary article which he wrote. General Arthur and his wife, whose home was near the Guards Training Battalion, had a particular gift for encouraging cadets and young officers, especially of his own Regiment. We felt part of his family (though the Coldstream has always had a strong family feeling) and we had an enormous respect for him as a soldier and as a Christian.

This new book will help SASRA by engendering interest and because it is a labour of love: all profits go to the work. It will also help many who are not connected with the Armed Forces, for Colonel Dobbie brings out clearly how a Christian may witness effectively for Christ within the confines of institutional life.

War is hateful but defence is vital, and the Armed Forces have served the Crown and the Nation well. It is worth remembering that traditional attitudes of the British Armed Services derive from Christian values. Whereas the armies of the ancient Romans and modern Nazis were based on fear, brutality and contempt for civilians, the British Armed Services are notable for comradeship, courtesy and compassion for the victims of war, disaster or famine.

But every serviceman and servicewoman needs the essential spark of Christian faith and the friendship of Christ, and in this respect SASRA's work is vital.

Rose Ash   JOHN POLLOCK
Devonshire
11th August 1987

FOREWORD to Second Edition

By

General Lord Dannatt of Keswick in the County of Norfolk GCB CBE MC

It is an enormous privilege to have been invited to write a Foreword to the revised edition of *Sovereign Service,* published to mark the 175th Anniversary of what is now the Soldiers' and Airmen's Scripture Readers Association. That fine Christian biographer, John Pollock, wrote the original Foreword which is quite properly retained in this new edition. Twenty five years on, the book has now been updated by the original author, Brigadier Ian Dobbie. For me, it is very special to share a publication with these two outstanding Christian warriors, who have both contributed so much to the spreading of the saving Gospel of our Lord Jesus Christ.

As this new volume describes, much has changed within the Armed Forces of the Crown in the last quarter of a century. At the time of the 150th Anniversary of SASRA in 1988 the conflict in Northern Ireland was unresolved and the Cold War showed no signs of thawing. Some might have despaired, some might have harboured a degree of hope, but others prayed. And the seemingly hopeless became reality; Northern Ireland is a much more peaceful place than before and the Berlin Wall is no more. The last twenty years have seen great changes for the Armed Forces – increased operational deployments to such places as Bosnia, Kosovo, East Timor, Sierra Leone, Iraq and Afghanistan – but nonetheless a further shrinkage in the size of the Royal Navy, the Army and the Royal Air Force. Sadly, the roll of honour of those who have lost their lives on operations, or suffered life-changing injuries, has increased with every deployment, especially Iraq and Afghanistan. But throughout all these changes, the work of presenting the truths and promises of Jesus Christ to the young men and women of the Army and the Royal Air Force through SASRA has flourished. This updated volume records the faithfulness of the Association to our calling, and the wonderful provision that our Heavenly Father has made for us to carry out that work.

In his original Foreword, John Pollock commented that "It is worth remembering that traditional attitudes of the British Armed Services derive from Christian values." Of course, he was absolutely right about that, but in our contemporary society where individualism flourishes, authority is challenged and social boundaries are pressed to the limit, even the Armed Forces have felt the winds of change. Mindful of this, a set of military core values was established and written down a decade or so ago. There are six: Selfless Commitment, Courage, Discipline, Loyalty, Integrity and Respect for Others. Unable to assume that recruits coming into our ranks today understand these things, they are now taught as a part of basic training, and refreshed annually as a standing requirement. Although they form a solid moral frame-work, they hold great spiritual truths as well. "Greater love has no one than this: to lay down one's life for one's friends" (John 15:13 TNIV). That Selfless Commitment was what Christ demonstrated on the first Good Friday and, rising from the dead, he broke the power of sin, guilt and death for all time for those who believe and trust in Him. Speaking of that military core value has provided a great opportunity for our Scripture Readers in recent years. And so has talking about Respect for Others. "My command is this: love each other as I have loved you." (John 15:12 TNIV). So, John Pollock was absolutely right about the attitudes of our military being derived from Christian values – the contemporary challenge has been to find new ways of presenting those everlasting values.

In its 175th year, SASRA has risen to that challenge and

these pages chronicle how this has been done. When, as legend has it, King George II rose to his feet during the singing of the Hallelujah Chorus at the conclusion of Handel's "Messiah" to acknowledge his service to the King of Kings, he set the theme and the underlying motivation of this book and our Association. We are in *Sovereign Service* to Her Majesty The Queen, our Patron, but we are in higher service to Almighty God, our King of Kings. Brigadier Ian Dobbie has set out an honest account of how we have sought to do our duty to God and Monarch over the last 175 years.

RICHARD DANNATT

General the Lord Dannatt GCB CBE MC
President, The Soldiers' and Airmen's Scripture Readers
Association
Constable, HM Tower of London

November 2012

PREFACE

The Council of The Soldiers' and Airmen's Scripture Readers Association has directed that the history of the Association should be published in 1988, which is in effect the 150th Anniversary of its being founded.

I have to confess that when I accepted responsibility for fulfilling this task I did not have much knowledge on which to draw. However, research soon revealed that some periods of the Association's history had been written already. These documents were generally produced anonymously, but are the property of the Association and in my judgement were written attractively and accurately. I did not feel that I could improve on them and decided to incorporate extracts in this production. Certainly some expressions were dated to the point of being quaint, and these I have changed; but I have endeavoured to do so in a way which captures the ideals, values and convictions of the original writers as I have sought to "weave them into a seamless robe".

Although a high proportion of this book is original, it would be more accurate to say that I have compiled this history rather than written it. Readers who are skilled in higher criticism will doubtless enjoy discerning which passages are entirely new!

This account has been written with an evangelical Christian readership in mind. Some may feel with justification that there are men and women who are worthy of mention who have been unaccountably omitted, particularly in the later part of the history. To these and their families I can only apologise, and plead that historical perspective is more easily achieved at a distance.

I am indebted to the Rev John Pollock and his publisher, John Murray, for allowing me to include a lengthy quotation from *Way to Glory*, a biography of Major General Sir Henry Havelock of Lucknow. I judge this to be the most inspiring biography of an evangelical Christian officer which it has been my privilege to read, and fervently hope that it will one day be republished. Although Havelock's influence on SASRA was indirect rather than direct, it was so massive that I felt it would have been remiss to exclude a major reference to his work and ministry of bringing the Gospel to soldiers of his day and generation.

My gratitude must also be extended to the Officers of the Corps of Royal Engineers for allowing me to include a photograph of the portrait of Her Majesty the Queen, their Colonel-in-Chief, which hangs in the dining room of the Headquarters Mess in Brompton Barracks at Chatham. The Officers' Christian Union have also kindly allowed me to use the memoir which I wrote in the magazine *Practical Christianity* on Lieutenant General Sir Arthur Smith in 1977 as an Appendix.

I must also thank those retired officers and others who have patiently read my drafts and made constructive criticisms and suggestions. These include Group Captain Alfred Knowles, Lieutenant Colonels Gerald Clarke, Tom Dick and Kenneth Sear, and Captain Sydney May and Mr John Diaper.

I own that I have found my task uplifting, heart-warming and challenging. This little volume is sent forth with humility and prayer that the reader will capture a fraction of that experience so that he is led to praise the Lord who brought SASRA into being; and consequently to nothing less than a prayerful interest in this noble missionary endeavour.

Havelock House
Barrack Road
Aldershot
April 1987

IAN DOBBIE
Colonel

CHAPTER 1

HISTORICAL REFLECTIONS AND INFLUENCES

It has been said that behind every movement of God there is a kneeling figure. There is no direct identification of the kneeling figure in the case of the Soldiers' and Airmen's Scripture Readers Association. It is hard to identify any obvious, direct, massive intercessor save the Captain of our Salvation who prayed in Gethsemane's garden for His apostles and also "for those who believe in Me through their word" (John 17:20). Additionally it is believed that early in the 19th century a group of Christian officers at the then War Office were praying for an organisation like the Association to come into being.

Military men have been evident among the believing people of God from Biblical times. In the Old Testament Joshua, Gideon and King David walked with God and drew strength from Him in their military responsibilities. During the Lord Jesus' earthly ministry and the apostolic age, Roman centurions and soldiers repented of sin and trusted Christ for salvation.

The first Christian to win a martyr's crown on English soil is believed to have been a Roman soldier named Alban. Centuries later during the English Civil War, many of Cromwell's soldiers held a simple Biblical faith, and were unashamed to acknowledge it publicly. We may be certain that some of these members of the Model Army will have soldiered (after the Restoration of the Monarchy) in the first standing army, which is regarded as the progenitor of the Regular Army we have today. Among the preachers many of these men would have heard or read would be Richard Baxter and John Bunyan, whose works have endured to our own day and generation. In Scotland, men of similar conviction were enlisted as soldiers into the Cameronians, "a psalm singing regiment" which was raised to guard the conventicles of the Field Preachers.

Inevitably soldiers were influenced during the evangelical awakening of the 18th century, when the Holy Spirit anointed the itinerant outdoor preachers such as George Whitfield and John Wesley. One of their colleagues, the Reverend Samuel Walker, witnessed no less than 200 soldiers from one regiment alone turn to Christ in 1756, during the nine weeks that they were billeted in Truro. The description of the parting of these soldiers from the evangelist who had ministered to them so faithfully makes affecting reading,[1] and will remind the reader of the Apostle Paul's farewell in Acts 20 to the young church at Ephesus.

The evangelical awakening influenced all classes, bringing with it a clear Biblical proclamation of the Gospel, a compassion for the needy, a sense of accountability and a desire among privileged men, especially those who had been spiritually regenerated, to serve God and their fellow men.

In the Peninsular War there were numbers of Christian officers and soldiers who met together for worship and mutual exhortation in cantonments, or in the field, seeking some secluded spot after the day's march was done. The Duke of Wellington referred to this in his dispatches, and stated that religious instruction is not only a moral necessity to every soul in the Army, but of the greatest support and aid to military discipline. He asked the authorities at home to send him a staff of "respectable clergymen" for in February 1811 there was only one chaplain in his Army. Thus simple Christian men influenced for good one of England's greatest military commanders who, in turn, took a spiritual initiative.

By the time the young Queen Victoria came to the throne in 1837, senior Christian officers, such as the Lawrence brothers, were beginning to show a spiritual concern for their men.

1. *Christian Leaders of the 18th Century* by J C Ryle, p.317.

It is against this backcloth that four impressive initiatives were taken by Christian laymen just before and during the Victorian age which were to have direct or indirect influence in the formation and work of The Soldiers' and Airmen's Scripture Readers Association which we know today. It is to these initiatives that the remainder of this chapter is devoted.

☆　☆　☆　☆　☆

SERGEANT RUDD

In 1804, a 28 year-old NCO in the Royal Artillery by the name of Rudd was posted to Woolwich. His influence under God was to be massive. Rudd started a Soldiers' Reading Room near the barracks to which godly men could go for reading, writing and devotional purposes. Supported by another NCO this work lasted for 26 years before the men who used it were posted to the Crimea.

However, the event for which Sergeant Rudd will be remembered with great gratitude occurred in 1816. In order to prosper the cause of the Gospel, Rudd displayed in the unit guardroom a notice offering to loan a Bible or Christian literature to any soldier who desired it. This courageous and commendable initiative, which gave Rudd numerous opportunities to help soldiers spiritually, was unfortunately taken without permission. He was reported, marched in front of his Commanding Officer, severely reprimanded, and threatened with an overseas posting!

These events came to the notice of a Christian officer at Woolwich by the name of Captain Maitland, who supported Rudd and was censured also. In the providence of God, Maitland was the son of a senior serving officer who reported the affair to the highest authority, with the consequence that a wagon load of Bibles was sent with orders that they be placed in every guardroom and hospital in The Garrison.

It is believed that this incident influenced the decision taken in 1825, and promulgated in King's Regulations, which authorised the issue at public expense of a Bible and Prayer Book to all who desired to have them, and directed that a stock be kept at depots for distribution to new recruits. In 1844 an order was published permitting these books to be retained on discharge from the Army. There is also evidence of a movement to enforce attendance at a regimental school by every recruit on joining to be taught to read. This enabled those who wished to do so to read their free issue Bible.

The provision of Bibles for individual soldiers was a great step forward, but until the problem of illiteracy was removed, additional measures needed to be taken to make Biblical truth available to soldiers. The Chaplain General, supported by Christian officers, gained permission to employ at their own expense literate, Christian ex-servicemen to go into barrack rooms to read the Scriptures to the troops. It is from this beginning that our evangelists get their title – Army, or at a later date Airmen's, Scripture Readers. The work continued until 1838 on this privately financed footing, and then the Soldiers' Friend Society was formed. This had a dual function, employing the Scripture Readers and what today we call deputation work, keeping the work in the public eye and raising support. It was later renamed The Army Scripture Readers Society. It is appropriate therefore to regard 1838 as the year of birth of what has become The Soldiers' and Airmen's Scripture Readers Association.

In 1856 the first War Office Charter for this work was drawn up, and it was under this authority, with its emphasis on permission to visit barrack rooms, hospital wards and detention barracks, that the work has been carried out since that time.

Sergeant Rudd's earthly pilgrimage ended in 1861 at the age of 85, but his life's work and influence has had a significance which continues to the present day.

☆　☆　☆　☆　☆

MAJOR GENERAL SIR HENRY HAVELOCK
OF LUCKNOW

No account of lay Christian witness within the military profession during the 19th century is complete without reference to General Havelock, whose statue stands next to Nelson's column in Trafalgar Square – the nation's tribute to his epic military leadership in the relief of Lucknow in 1857.

Born in 1795, the son of a prosperous shipbuilder, Henry Havelock was educated at Charterhouse, the same school as John Wesley. Following calamitous failure in the family business, Havelock became a soldier and was commissioned into the Rifle Brigade in 1815. Service abroad offered opportunities to achieve financial benefit through promotion without purchase, so Havelock transferred to the Somerset Light Infantry and sailed for India in 1823, impecunious and dissatisfied.

During the course of the sea voyage a brother officer named James Gardner ("a humble, unpretending man") lent Havelock two Christian biographies and led him through the Biblical passages which show why Christ died. Havelock had never understood before that this sacrifice of God's Son had been made in order to redeem sinners like himself. He realised that this amazing love demanded a response. Havelock counted the cost of discipleship, aware that he might well be ostracised by his fellow officers, and before the end of the sea voyage put his trust in Christ alone for salvation. This conversion experience revolutionised his life. He married the daughter of an English missionary and decided, in his own words, "as a solemn Christian duty" to devote his free time and attention to the spiritual welfare of his men. The one chaplain in the station was responsible for the troops and European civilians, and his spiritual oversight could not be more than nominal. Havelock decided to hold informal meetings for such men as were "well disposed". Other officers in the Regiment, except Gardner and the judicious Commanding Officer Robert Sale, were appalled at this initiative as they feared that, even in the hands of so respected an officer as Havelock, such meetings would be subversive of discipline. But Havelock's mind was set. The following moving account of his spiritual work among soldiers is quoted from his biography by J. C. Pollock in *Way to Glory*.

"Havelock, though a mere subaltern again, was working far harder than most, and for a definite purpose: 'It was the great object of my ambition to be surpassed by none in zeal and determination in the path of my duty, because I was resolved to put down the vile calumny that a Christian could not be a meritorious soldier.'

"The 13th Light Infantry was made up of drafts typical of the recruits which England despatched to the East – the refuse of London streets and jails. When Havelock had first re-joined indiscipline was rife, officers were stabbed and Lieutenant Colonel Sale, the commanding Officer, was once shot at. Again and again the regiment would attend punishment parade to see a man strapped to the triangle, naked to the waist, to receive two or three hundred lashes. Sale won through and by the time they reached Agra the 13th were reported by the divisional general 'one of the finest corps I have seen in India; and its very high state of discipline does great credit to the zeal and ability of its commanding officer'.

"Off duty the men were treated as in any other regiment – serfs to be fed and housed, but not otherwise the responsibility of their officers. In the hot weather, parades were early in the morning and in the evening; during the heat of the day, from nine to five, the unmarried men were confined to their barrack rooms and verandas with nothing to do, most not even knowing how to read.

"Liquor was cheap and plentiful, and though the ration in the canteen was strong enough more could be obtained from native vendors or unscrupulous sergeants' wives, drunkenness thus being the commonest crime. When not drinking, many would wander into the bazaar to frequent the houses of ill-fame where low-caste women were ready to satisfy the lusts of men whose blood was stirred by the warm climate. The policy of placing in one barrack room men of varying ages and service made it difficult for a young soldier to retain any high ideals. As a private of the 13th wrote a few years later, 'In many instances the lips of both sergeant and private teemed alike with pollution, and their horrible oaths and execrations coupled with expressions of obscenity pained my ears tenfold more than the shrill screaming of the troops of jackals that came nightly from the graves and tombs to prey upon the offal of the camp.' There was one custom which inevitably degraded. Every week the doctor went the rounds of the barrack rooms and held an inspection for venereal disease, mere lads and hardened lechers alike parading stripped, each being examined in the frankest manner in sight of the rest.

"With men under such conditions Havelock re-started his Bible meetings. A few survived of his earlier group, the chief being a sergeant, George Godfrey. Not unnaturally Godfrey and his fellows followed their leader into Baptist allegiance, and at Dinapore they had built a makeshift chapel. At Agra, Havelock decided on a more permanent structure and Godfrey 'collected a great deal of money for the new chapel from officers and men of the 13th and residents' while Havelock endowed it by buying land at Chitaurah, twenty miles away, which he cleared with convict labour borrowed from the magistrate, and then leased.[2]

"The small group of thoroughgoing Christians met daily for hymn-singing, Bible reading and prayer. The chapel also provided an opportunity, not then otherwise allowed for in a military cantonment, of 'small places for retirement for private devotion, to which many resort,' as Havelock wrote to Dr Marsham in Serampore. On Sundays, after the men had attended the obligatory church parade service, 'there is public worship before noon, and in the evening. I think,' continued Havelock, 'the congregation on the latter occasion fluctuates between fifty and sixty, sometimes however, exceeding this latter number; and it is admitted that ... the frequenters of this chapel are reckoned among the best behaved men in the regiment.'

"At his chapel services Havelock was content for a while to read a printed sermon of some contemporary divine, but this seemed 'a spiritless action, which does not move and awaken as does the declaration of his own views in an address indicted by the speaker', and he began to write and read out

2. It is still the property of the Baptist Missionary Society. The chapel is now known as Havelock's Chapel.

his own sermons – a clear break from the stiffly regulated conventions of the early nineteenth century. He found that 'the men listen gladly'.

"His personal efforts were limited to his soldiers. And thus young men who had almost forgotten childhood attendance in an English country church, or who since earliest days in slum streets had never had the chance of hearing the Christian Gospel, would risk the ribaldry of their friends and take a seat at the back of the chapel on a Sunday evening.

"The palm-mats were rolled up and the room open to the hot still air. Round the walls vegetable oil lamps guttered and flickered. The singing and prayers done, the men sat stiff and erect. Havelock spoke. He knew what they needed and told them in clipped, simple phrases: 'Time is short, and eternity at hand,' he would begin, and the men remembered the dozen or more of their comrades buried in the past six or nine months, 'so I must not delay to speak to you on the most important of all subjects – the care and prospects of your immortal souls. Do not suffer yourself to be deceived by the false names which men give to things; but look steadily at the abiding truth, that mankind are divided into two classes – the children of God, and the servants of the world and its prince Satan. Make at once your choice for that good part which shall not hereafter be taken from you. Come to the Lord Jesus Christ, and ask Him for instruction and enlightenment of mind, and change of heart; and then do all that He commands you, and you shall be happy for ever … Learn to regard Jesus Christ as personally your Friend and Benefactor, to come to Him for all that you need, to feel assured that all your sins are laid on Him …'

"When the service was over he would, if a man so desired, speak with him individually, showing from his Bible the way in which he might 'have Jesus for your Friend'. For those moments the relationship of officer and ranker was forgotten, to be resumed inexorably when they left the chapel.

"Havelock's constant work in spare time was costly for his wife, who once remarked to her mother that 'Henry is at his office all the morning and I do enjoy his society so much when he comes home that I am quite jealous of the time he spends among his soldiers'. But she gave him all support in her power, starting a Sunday school for the regiment's children, teaching the men to read, and encouraging

19

Havelock when his chapel was the target of violent criticism. 'I trust,' she wrote, 'that my dear Henry will be spared to continue to use all his efforts to be useful to the soldiers, among whom he is greatly beloved.'

"For all this voluntary service for the welfare of his men was done, so Havelock wrote, 'in the very teeth of ridicule and opposition.' Officers of the 13th, though acknowledging Havelock pleasant enough a man with a good record of soldiering, considered that he was making himself ridiculous. Nor did criticism come only from the empty-headed topers such as were to be found in every mess at a time when the only antidote for heat and boredom was believed to be brandy. The gossip went round and round and when, in their absence, officers and their wives were discussing the Havelocks they were able, as so often in religious controversies, to summon considerable moral indignation: Havelock did not receive pay in order to interfere with the private lives of the men – his constant consorting with them was bound to subvert discipline and put notions in their heads – he demeaned himself by social intercourse with his inferiors – for a King's officer not to belong to the Established Church smacked of disloyalty; and as for a layman preaching and conducting services, it was thoroughly unseemly. He should stick to the work for which he was paid, and leave the men to see to their own amusements. And thus a course of action which to later generations appeared commendable was criticized in the pioneer.

"One couple alone stood quietly for Havelock – Robert Sale his commanding officer and Florentia his masterful and determined wife. Sale, indeed, though not following Havelock in all things, was thoroughly content with him, as he showed on one occasion in no uncertain manner. When Havelock once was ill, a 'saint', one of his own company, was reported drunk, to the merriment and jubilations of the critics. On return to duty Havelock demanded an investigation before the Commanding Officer. His man was produced and he had no difficulty in proving that the defaulter was of the same name in another company. The accusers thereupon shifted their ground and illogically complained that the fellow was a Baptist anyway, at which Sale lost his temper, thumped the table (the story was told all over India) and exclaimed, 'Baptists! Baptists! I know nothing about Baptists. But I know that I wish the whole regiment were Baptists. Their names are never in the defaulters' roll and they are never in the guardroom.'

"While at Agra Havelock took a step which had far-reaching result. He and his men had chafed at the compulsory church parades which, by the Articles of War, Roman Catholics were excused while Dissenters were not. In October 1832 Havelock drew up a Memorandum to the Commander-in-Chief at the Horse Guards petitioning that the liberty accorded Roman Catholics in the Army be extended to Dissenters. Sale forwarded the Memorandum to the Governor-General and in due course it reached London and for seven years filtered through the appropriate channels until in July 1839 Havelock's request led to liberty of worship for the whole British Army."

Havelock's influence during and after his lifetime (he died at Lucknow shortly after the epic relief in 1857) was deep and lasting. Between his death and world War I no one seriously maintained that it was impossible to profess "to fear God as well as honour the Queen ... that no man could at once be described by Lord Hardinge: "Every inch a soldier; and every inch a Christian".

"The friendship of Christ was Havelock's secret and remains his message: 'It is a happy thing beyond description to have a Heavenly Father and a powerful Friend in whom to put our trust.'"

It is not surprising that the Headquarters of The Soldiers' and Airmen's Scripture Readers Association is named "Havelock House", a testimony to the faithfulness of God in raising up an officer of great military distinction who achieved so much of spiritual benefit for his soldiers.

☆　☆　☆　☆　☆

MISS LUCY DEACON

Students of evangelistic endeavour among servicemen in the 19th century cannot fail to be impressed at the fruitful ministry of Christian women in this field of Service. Dame

21

Agnes Weston launched the Royal Sailors' Rests hostels; Mrs Daniell and her daughter opened up Soldiers' Homes, the first being in Aldershot; Miss Sandes initiated a similar work with homes opening up in the Far East and India as well as in Britain; Mrs Todd Osborne in Scotland was led of God to begin identical work which spread into the Mediterranean and Middle East, and became known as the Mission to the Mediterranean Garrisons (now the Mission to Military Garrisons). These ladies were from families of high social standing, and ministered in an age when it was not fashionable for women to play a prominent part in leadership in any field. Their service was costly; they faced the scorn and sneers of their peers. Had they not been called of God to this selective and specialised mission field, they would not have had the resolve of faith to maintain their course of service. It is a glowing testimony to their obedience to their Heavenly Master, that the work of each of these women continues today over 100 years after it was launched; and during that time a steady trickle of men and women have come to faith in Christ through this work. To this list of gallant and noble Christian ladies the name of Miss Lucy Deacon can be added without reserve.

Miss Deacon came from a godly family of Christian bankers. It was natural therefore that they should support such evangelistic endeavours as the missions led by the American Dwight L Moody. Moody had been a simple shoe salesman in Chicago, whom the Lord had raised up to become an international evangelist. His ministry in Britain was prolific.[3] All types and conditions of men, even university scholars, were influenced by this unlettered but humble servant of God. It was at one of his missions in London in 1883 that he made a remark to which Lucy Deacon responded with long term effect. As he surveyed the crowds flocking into Exeter Hall one day, Moody asked Miss Deacon to go and sit among the substantial number of soldiers who attended each night in uniform. He had gathered round him a band of workers drawn from many walks of life, and, like the wise leader he was, he meant to

3. *Moody without Sankey* by J C Pollock is recommended reading

make the best possible disposition of the forces at his command.

In the vast audience were all sorts of conditions of men, gathered together by a common impulse, eager to see something of this gifted messenger of God, and to hear what he had to say which might help them in their particular difficulties. Business men would best be helped by those who daily were facing commercial problems, and solving them in the light of their saving knowledge of Christ; artisans, grappling with the question of feeding growing families on low wages, could best be assisted by those of their own class who had become "more than conquerors" through their simple trust in God.

But this "thin red line" of soldiers, who had become so striking a feature of the meetings, as they sat night after night in the front row, called for prayerful consideration. Moody had given the matter a good deal of thought. These men were, by the very nature of their calling, cut off to a large extent from the refining influences of womanhood. On the other hand, their lives were lived more under the constant notice of their fellows then the majority of those present.

Each man knew, moreover, that if he made a public profession of conversion at Exeter Hall, the news would possibly reach barracks before he himself got there. To bring them to that point of decision, therefore, needed special care. The gentle word of a woman might well prove to be the factor which would decide the issue in the battle within them. That word must, however, be spoken by one on whose judgement the leader could rely, and to whom the soldiers would give respectful attention.

Moody's somewhat abrupt suggestion to Miss Deacon was one which tested the depth of the consecration of the young lady to whom it was addressed. Tradition and the social conventions of Victorian society were all against such activities – whether religious or political – and those who disregarded these conventions were looked upon with suspicion, and even disapproval, by the majority of their friends. Moreover, in all classes of society the private soldier was considered to be the least desirable company for respectable young women. Yet here was a lady of culture and refinement being invited to take her place in the middle of a row of "Redcoats" in one of the most conspicuous parts of the building.

That moment in Exeter Hall was a critical one, not only for Miss Deacon, but also for countless men whose lives she later influenced. Had she declined the suggestion, few of her contemporaries would have blamed her, but thousands of men, whose lives have been transformed through faith in the Crucified and Risen Lord, might have missed receiving the help they needed. But Miss Deacon responded, and from that act of consecration there sprang the work which later become known all over the Empire as The Soldiers' and Airmen's Christian Association.

For a moment she hesitated; but that moment of hesitation was to have its value for the years that lay ahead. Years later the scene was still vividly impressed upon her mind. Miss Deacon recorded how dismayed she felt, and how in that moment of need, she prayed. During those days many eloquent prayers had ascended from Exeter Hall, but none could have been more heartfelt than that unspoken cry to God, and few can have had a more abundant answer. As she stood there, she saw her cousin who, like herself, had come prepared to undertake any soul-winning service that might be asked of her. Miss Deacon beckoned to her, and a few moments later the two helpers took their places beside a group of Guardsmen from Wellington Barracks.

It is doubtful if these soldiers knew what they were seeking. Humanly speaking, it would have seemed improbable that two cultured young women, who had never spoken to a soldier before, would be able to lead them to faith in the Lord Jesus Christ. These two consecrated helpers knew however that they could do all things through Christ who would strengthen them, and soon they were the means of persuading scores of men to make their way into the enquiry room during Moody's campaign. Furthermore, they were the means of helping many a soldier to win others for the Saviour – a simple New Testament policy which is still at the heart of the Association's evangelistic work.

During Moody's meetings, Miss Deacon and her cousin were not called upon to do more than speak a word of encouragement to those of the men who appeared to be impressed by the address. There were experienced workers in the enquiry rooms who were able to give any further help that might be necessary. But it was not long before they were called upon to follow up the work which they had begun. A few days after the first group of converts had been registered, a message was received by Miss Deacon, telling her that Moody was anxious that she and her cousin should take a parcel of books to each convert in barracks, make enquiries as to his progress, and give such encouragement as they were able. Once more, all the restrictions of the period were against such a course. The visits had to be made publicly. The workers had to call at the barrack gates, hand in the list of those whom they wished to see, and wait until they were sent for. From these visits and contacts, there sprang into being a small meeting for Christian soldiers which was held in the back room of a house in Vauxhall Bridge Road; and it was from this meeting that The Soldiers' Christian Association originated and grew.

However it was later and amid other surroundings that it took definite shape. In the pleasant garden of Miss Deacon's home in South London, a dozen or more soldiers, who had been influenced for Christ during the Moody Revival, were gathered for prayer and Bible study. The question of uniting in some way all those in the Army who were seeking to witness for Christ had been discussed. This new idea was one which needed considerable thought, and was the subject of much prayer. There was a certain amount of criticism and even opposition; but the seed sown in that garden grew and flourished under the guiding hand of God.

☆　☆　☆　☆　☆

W B HARRINGTON

Twenty years before Miss Deacon had invited those Guardsmen into the enquiry room at Exeter Hall, a springless, bullock-drawn hospital wagon might have been seen slowly rattling along the dusty road from Peshawar to Mooltan. After leaving Lahore, the road stretched drearily across the plains, and there was little sign of life upon it other than the lean, grey "tree-rats" and the drowsy coolie sitting on the front of the wagon, automatically grunting at the patient beasts harnessed to it. Every mile of that journey was agony for the young man who lay on the hard, straw palliasse in the wagon, and every jolt was mental torture to his brave wife who watched untiringly by his side.

Mr W B Harrington, a young official in the Public Works Department of the Indian Government, was on his way to his new station. He was keen on his work, and keen to win men for Christ; and at every halting place on his journey he heard stories of the character of the regiment ahead of him, who were also marching from Agra to Mooltan, after three years of almost unbelievable experience in that province.

In the critical years that followed the Mutiny, the regiment had been constantly on the move, and had been unable to obtain any of the very scanty supply of clothing that was available in India. In 1859, 300 survivors marched into Agra, but with little of the traditional smartness of the British soldier about them. There were no smart uniforms, shining buttons, nor pipeclayed gloves. Many were coatless; all were in rags; and some wore rice bags, with holes cut for arms and legs, while their boots were tied with string.

The men themselves were as wild as they looked, for they had been separated from moral and spiritual restraints throughout all those terrible months. It is no wonder that many of them during the two years of comparative civilisation which followed, entered into every kind of dissipation that was open to them and became notorious for their excesses. An outbreak of cholera failed to sober them, but it necessitated a change of station, and so came the order for the march to Mooltan. It was a severe test of their physical endurance and discipline, for every step of those 250 miles was over ill-made roads, ankle-deep in dust, with the supply of water scanty and not too clean. And if little was done for their physical well-being, less was attempted for their spiritual needs. As one of them wrote, long after: "Truly no man cared for our souls."

The sick man and his wife who followed heard stories of their drunkenness and crimes of violence. The wife must often have trembled at the prospect ahead, but she said nothing of her fears, and joined with her husband in his prayer that it might be possible to do something for God among the "rough lot" with whom they were to share their new station.

Men from that regiment must have seemed unlikely candidates for Christianity, but these two devoted Christians had seen, during their brief career among the troops, what the grace of God could accomplish in the lives of men. They had seen hard, careless, godless men transformed into good soldiers of Jesus Christ as well as of their Queen, and they believed that what God had done elsewhere, He would do at Mooltan.

Wherever he had gone, Harrington had seen the great need for a place where men who were witnessing for Christ, or who sought to know more about the Christian life, could gather for study, prayer and meditation. His work as a constructional engineer who was often engaged in the erection of barracks, and his concern for the men who occupied them, combined to fire him with a great desire to establish such a place in every military station throughout India. From time to time he had been able to secure the temporary use of buildings as prayer rooms, but it was at Mooltan that he saw the first step towards the realisation of his dreams – the opening of the first permanent prayer room in India.

There is a definite link between the scene on the Mooltan road and the crowded meeting at Exeter Hall, for the young man who was so determined to do what he could to help the "roughest lot in India" was one of the first most enthusiastic supporters of The Soldiers' Christian Association, and remained one of its most untiring and successful workers until well after his eightieth birthday.

Very soon after Harrington's arrival in Mooltan, it was announced that a meeting would be held in the house of an officer of the Royal Artillery. All preparations were made: one man turned up! A little later, another meeting was arranged, this time in Harrington's bungalow. Again everything was ready. A long table was placed down the centre of the well-lit room, and Bibles and hymn-books provided. Only one man turned up. He was rather shy, but appreciated the kindly greeting, the words of welcome and cheer, and the simple prayer. The next day he came again, bringing another man with him. These two brought another two, and by the end of the week the room began to fill. Month after month, the Gospel story was unfolded to these rough men. Results soon became evident in two ways. Officers as well as their comrades saw evidence of changed characters and in the men themselves there arose a keen desire to read the Word of God.

This created another problem. The majority of soldiers in those days were quite illiterate; only a few could read. This did not trouble them while they were content with the usual pleasures that life in India had to offer them; but once they had come to put their trust in Christ they longed to grow spiritually and to know more of Christ from Scripture. Instruction in reading and writing was therefore essential, and there was none to provide this but these devoted servants of God. It was hard work, but the pupils were eager. To these men, more accustomed to marching, fighting and digging than to gentler tasks, the weight of a quill pen was more onerous than all their equipment. Those who have seen the struggles of grown men, who have never been schooled, seeking to master the mysteries of the alphabet, will realise the hours of toil and mental anguish that these lessons involved.

The "rough lot" were finding the way to better things.

But the prayer room was not yet built, and the soldiers who knew something of the ways of government departments in those times would express concern for arrangements in other stations when postings occurred. The need drove Harrington to increased prayer and effort, and on 3rd March 1864 the corner-stone of the first permanent prayer room in India was laid. Engraved in that stone is an inscription which states that the object of the building was "to further the cause of Christ in the Army, and to promote the spiritual welfare of all who may resort to it"; and that it was "founded in believing prayer, that, by the blessing of God, many within these walls might be brought to know their Saviour, and to build upon Him as the Chief Corner-Stone." The building was completed and publicly dedicated on 23rd December 1864. Within a few months of its completion, the man who God had raised up to establish it was transferred to another station.

A year later, the second prayer room was erected at Rawalpindi, and applications had been made for sites at other stations. The Viceroy and Governor-General[4] became interested, and, as a result of the correspondence which followed his inquiries, an Order in Council was issued to the effect that:

> "Taking into consideration the difficulties and inconveniences experienced by pious and well-disposed soldiers of British regiments, owing to the want of some place of retirement for prayer and reading God's Word, and for holding prayer and other meetings of a devotional character, the Right Honourable the Governor-General in Council has determined that a room of a suitable size, with such furniture as may be deemed necessary to fit it for the purposes above mentioned, shall be considered one of the recognized requirements of every British regiment or considerable detachment of troops."

Those who had experience of life in a military station in India acknowledged the wisdom of this decision; and

4. This was Lord Lawrence, brother of Sir Henry Lawrence who was resident at Lucknow and died there prior to the relief by Generals Havelock and Outram in 1857. All four of these men were devoted Christians.

throughout the succeeding years the prayer rooms provided a place in barracks where men could draw aside to meet with God, to learn more of Him through the study of His Word, and to have fellowship one with another. The prayer engraved on the corner-stone was abundantly answered.

During his years of service in India, Harrington gave himself unceasingly to the task of winning soldiers for Christ, and to the ministry of establishing them in the faith. When the news of the formation of the SCA reached him, he was delighted and threw himself wholeheartedly into the task of organising it in India. Without delay, Harrington undertook the formation of branches in almost every British unit of the Army in India.

God's Word assures Christians that they who sow in tears shall reap in joy, and such was the outcome of this pioneer effort. In spite of many changes within the Army in India, the work was maintained on a high level of spiritual efficiency; and it is encouraging to record that the Indian Government directed that the numerous prayer rooms of the Association should be known as " Harrington Prayer Rooms" in memory of that consecrated servant of Jesus who was "not disobedient to the heavenly vision".

☆　☆　☆　☆　☆

SUMMARY

This first chapter has highlighted some of the lay Christians whose ministry was so influential among soldiers in the 19th century in particular. This list is obviously not comprehensive; not least because no mention is made of the many men and women known to God alone, who prayed devotedly and continuously for such work, nor of the Commanders and Chaplains who so graciously gave support and encouragement. However, focus has been placed on those who were used to act as spiritual midwives in the birth of The Army Scripture Readers Society, and The Soldiers' Christian Association.

The next three chapters will relate the story of their respective ministries in the early years and of how amalgamation took place in 1938 to form The Soldiers' and Airmen's Scripture Readers Association we know today.

CHAPTER 2

THE ARMY SCRIPTURE READERS

THE FIRST HUNDRED YEARS

We have already seen how The Soldiers' Friend and Army Scripture Readers Society came into being. Its objectives were the propagation of the Christian Gospel throughout the Army, primarily by personal evangelism in barrack rooms, but also by the distribution of Bibles, tracts and devotional books, the establishment of reading rooms and libraries, and prayer meetings amongst soldiers, both inside and outside of barracks. From its earliest days the Society determined not to interfere with the denominational liberty of the soldiers, but sought to fulfil the most noble of all aims – "to bring soldiers to a saving knowledge of Christ".

In addition to Scripture Readers, from about 1838 two agents were appointed and visits were made to barracks at Brighton, Chatham, Exeter, Gravesend, Hounslow, Ipswich, Windsor, Woolwich and all units in London. For 21 years the work progressed steadily and unobtrusively with little variation. From the earliest days God honoured this humble ministry. Thousands of men were contacted annually, and reports reveal individual soldiers repenting of sin and trusting Christ. In their turn these young Christians sought to influence their comrades for Christ, and a witness led by Christian laymen spread to the garrisons of Canada and the Mediterranean, producing transformation of life, enlargement of vision and the increase of missionary activity.

In 1859 The Soldiers' Friend and Army Scripture Readers Society amalgamated, with the unanimous consent of both committees, with another organisation

Maj. Gen. Sir Henry Havelock, KCB
"Havelock of Lucknow"

Miss L. S. J. Deacon
Foundress of the Soldiers' Christian
Association 1st January 1887

Mr. W. B. Harrington
Instrumental in establishing the first of many "Prayer Rooms" in India
in 1864 for use of the soldiers serving there.

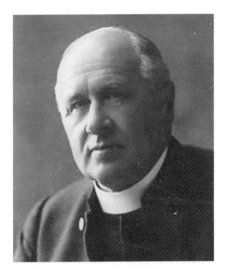

Bishop Taylor-Smith, KCB, CVO, DD
Chaplain General to the Forces 1901-1925

Capt. W. H. Dawson
Benefactor of ASR & SFS and SCA

Mr. G. J. Byrnell
Secretary SCA 1916-1931

Capt. A. L. Perry, MBE, MC
Secretary SACA 1931-1938
Secretary ASR and SACA 1938-1948

Col. S. D. Cleeve, CB
Secretary ASR and SFS 1908-1934

Lt. Col. R. K. A. Macaulay, DSO
Secretary ASR and SFS 1934-1936
General Secretary ASR & SFS and SACA 1936-1938
General Secretary ASR and SACA 1938-1949

Headquarters May 1926

Top Row: *C. Jackson, T. Buchan, C. Coupland, A. C. Cooper.*

Centre Row: *Ben Johnson, R. Smart, W. G. Ransley, T. Hopkins,
H. A. Wisbey, R. Oliver, H. G. Howell.*

Front Row: *A. E. Steward, F. Burgess, A. McEvitt,
P. Gibbon, Ben Wood, MBE, F. Yearsley, S. Smallbrook, W. E. Gould,
A. L. Whitcher.*

In the doorway: *Col. S. W. Cleeve (Gen. Sec.) Partially obscured by
ASR A. Smart, Capt. Allen Cooper (Deputation Sec.), P. G. Sargeant
(collar only visible).*

In between back row: *Between T. Buchan and C. Coupland,
G. J. G. Howard (Sec. for Ireland); between C. Coupland and
A. C. Cooper, Rev. Sir Montague Beauchamp, Bt (Clerical Deputation Sec.).*

Mr. W. B. Harrington and
Seaforth Highlanders SCA Branch Murree, India 1897

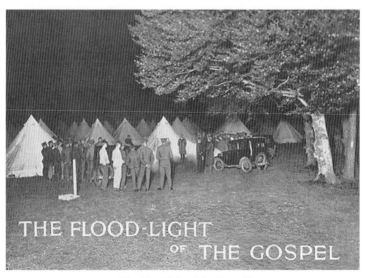

THE FLOOD-LIGHT
OF THE GOSPEL

"The Floodlight of the Gospel"
An SACA Open-Air Meeting at night on Salisbury Plain
using car headlights.

Major Lee Spratt
SCA Representative, India 1919-1927
ASR and SACA Representative, India 1938-1945

Capt. H. S. May
Asst. Secretary ASR and SACA 1945-1951
Asst. Secretary SASRA 1951-1968

Lt. Gen. Sir William Dobbie, GCMG, KCB, DSO
President ASR & SACA 1947-1950
President SASRA 1950-1967

Lt. Gen. Sir Arthur Smith, KCB, KBE, DSO, MC, LLD
President 1967-1977, Chairman 1948-1967

called the British Army Scripture Readers Society. History does not relate how this latter organisation came into being, but it is evident that it did not enjoy the confidence of chaplains or military authorities. The amalgamation appears to have been wise and achieved an increased efficiency of this type of Christian work in the Army.

Among those who will have been especially glad to have seen this new structure was the Chaplain General himself, the Reverend G R Gleig. He had been convinced for some time of the need for Scripture Readers and had already sought to initiate another scheme himself! However, he had faced opposition from military authorities also, as his own account reveals:

"For some years I was a little fearful of lay interference in the religious proceedings of the Army ... and years ago, I will not say how many, I myself drew up a plan for the introduction of Scripture Readers in the Army. I submitted it to the Archbishop of Canterbury ... I then went with it in my hand to the military authorities, ... my proposals were not met with a very cordial spirit, and therefore, feeling myself powerless to do good, I thought there was no occasion whatever for me to run the risk of doing evil, and I was silent ... and held aloof till one day we were waited upon at the War Office by a deputation of gentlemen of high rank in the Army, who proposed that as the Soldiers' Friend Society had not obtained – I do not say had justly not obtained – the confidence of the authorities, it would be right for the Army itself to form a Soldiers' Friend Society. They brought me the rules and regulations which they proposed, and I accepted them, thanking God that such an opportunity had offered itself.

"Then later, as it appeared that both societies were seeking the same great end (ie, to spread the saving knowledge of Christ amongst our soldiers), there arose between them a series of negotiations, which being conducted on both sides in a most Christian spirit, at last ended (after three years) in the happy union of which I am appointed this day to be the representative ...

"Let me now explain the principles of action upon which I hope and believe that from this time the affairs of the United Association will be conducted.

33

"Remember that it is a very delicate matter to interfere with what is called military discipline; and that most earnest minded men may bring about the greatest mischief if they permit their zeal to outrun their judgement. I say, therefore, this Society will do its best work if it throws itself frankly, honestly and without reserve into all those arrangements which are absolutely necessary to preserve goodwill in the Army. I want to see our Army Scripture Readers go hand in hand with the clergy wherever they find them.

"We have now a large staff of Army Chaplains ... our Army Scripture Readers must consider themselves co-labourers with them, subordinate to them, resorting to them for direction and advice ... I will never countenance any attempt at proselytism ... I won't have the Scripture Readers making war upon the Roman Catholics, because I think they will have plenty of work to do in making the Protestant members of our great Army Christians in name and in deed."

From this time onwards the records show that the united society became, in God's hands, an instrument of doing more good amongst the soldiers of the British Army than had yet been accomplished.

The management was now entrusted to a General Committee of 48, namely 26 officers, 6 laymen and 16 Army Chaplains of various denominations. Thus the work developed and was extended to embrace the whole Army, and Lieutenant General Sir Arthur J Lawrence was appointed President of the newly amalgamated Society, with Colonel Robert Pitcairn and Mr W A Blake as joint Secretaries, with the original Headquarters in Trafalgar Square.

Some years later the Committee was reduced to 24, namely 18 officers (as many as possible to be still serving) and 6 Army Chaplains of various denominations. The Headquarters was then in St Martin's Lane for many years, and moved to "Havelock House" in 1925, when the freehold of the building was presented as a gift to the Society by the late Captain W H Dawson, late Inniskilling Dragoons. A dedication service was held on 25th May 1925 by Bishop J Taylor Smith (Chaplain General of the Army from 1901 to 1925).

On 26th May 1892, Field Marshal Lord Wolseley, then Commander-in-Chief, Ireland, succeeded Sir Arthur Lawrence as President of the Society and, after his death in 1913, King George V graciously agreed to become Patron and was supported by Field Marshal The Duke of Connaught.

Reading accounts of the initiative and changes in structure in the 19th century with the benefit of hindsight, it is natural to ask whether the military authorities were instinctively hostile to the witness of simple Christians like Scripture Readers, or whether those who pioneered this work matched their zeal for the Gospel with wisdom and courtesy. It would probably be fair to deduce that mistakes were made by all parties at some time or another. Authority did not share the same priorities as the Readers, and these men and their committees did not always understand the just concern of commanders to ensure that discipline and good order were maintained, and that these officers had a keen sense of professional accountability. The provision of the War Office Charter in 1856, the amalgamation of societies with identical ideals and the wise counsel of successive Chaplains General in the early years did much to reduce misunderstandings in later generations. And it was a Chaplain General, speaking at the amalgamated society's annual meeting in Exeter Hall in the 1880s, who issued the Readers of his day and generation with a memorable and clear directive which is as apposite today as it was on the day it was delivered:

> "The Scripture Readers are to proclaim Christ, and Christ alone. They are to go forth to preach and live Christ; they are to hold up Christ as everything. Christ the atonement for sin; Christ working through the blessed Spirit. They are to hold up to men Christ the Captain of their Salvation, Christ the Leader, Christ the Forerunner, Christ the Example, Christ the Hope of Humanity. They are to preach and live Christ. They are not to trouble themselves about other matters. This Society does not wish them to go forth to

find fault with this or that kind of service (not to proselytise; they have nothing to do with that!). Their work is to proclaim Christ, as Christ must be proclaimed by men who have 'Christ in them the hope of glory'. I am thoroughly agreed with these principles of this society, which are, as the Report says, of God."

☆　☆　☆　☆　☆

SCRIPTURE READERS ON ACTIVE SERVICE

At the beginning of the Crimean War in 1854, an advertisement was put into the Illustrated London News, asking for donations to help seven Scripture Readers to be sent out to the war. The response was encouraging, for the subscriptions which followed enabled 13 Readers to be sent out and these men shared the hardships of the British soldiers on active service in the Crimean campaign. Allies were not forgotten as one of the Readers was appointed to work among Protestants in the French forces. It is interesting to note that unusually he was an ordained man, the Reverend Alexander Levis, and not an ex-soldier. We must assume that he was appointed on the grounds that it had not been easy to find a conventional Scripture Reader with a fluent knowledge of French.

Russian prisoners from the war were transported to England, and the Society provided them with Gospels and tracts in Russian as well as appointing a Russian-speaking Scripture Reader. We know nothing of this man or how, in the providence of God, he had acquired the necessary knowledge of Russian.

One Crimean Reader's diary reveals a passion for souls on the part of the man himself: hard, long treks, laden with copies of the Scriptures for dissemination among the troops and an iron will which kept a weaker constitution going amidst exposure to weather, disease, and other difficulties common to active service. The diary closes on 10th June 1855, but we have a glimpse of another Reader's work from the diary of Captain Hedley Vicars who won the Victoria Cross:

"How glad I shall be to see the Soldier's missionary, Duncan Matheson! It will refresh and cheer my soul. Oh, that there were many more labourers in this harvest! Why are there not more Scripture Readers sent out? They are grievously wanted here ..."

Later he was to write:

"On return to my tent, who should I find but Mr Duncan Matheson, the Soldier's missionary from Balaclava. He remained with me for about an hour, and I do not think I ever enjoyed a more heavenly conversation than with this man of God. We read the third Chapter of Ephesians, and he prayed with me. When he left, I saw that three of my brother officers were standing close by; they must have heard that fervent prayer. Who knows but that one of them may be led to pray for himself tonight? God grant it."

Among others who took a deep interest in the work of the Readers at that time was the heroic Florence Nightingale. In 1861 she sent a generous donation to support the work of the Readers, and continued to do so for a further 24 years, her letters being described as "couched in the kindest of terms".

In 1868 two Readers accompanied the Abyssinian Expedition, and received great help and encouragement from the senior officers in command, and two more served in the Zululand campaign of 1879 and were given the opportunity to bring God's Word to men in danger and difficulty.

When the belated force set off in 1884 to go up the Nile to relieve Khartoum, an ex-Gordon Highlander was sent out at very short notice as a Scripture Reader. On reaching Cairo he found that the expedition was leaving next day by river, but the local Army authorities knew nothing about him. However, through prayer and persistence, he got a permit and set off with a convoy of ten boats. It was desperately hard work, because when the wind was adverse, the boats had to be man-handled and rowed. At night, when they anchored, blistered hands and aching bones made sleep, in the warm sand, difficult. In the warm darkness the Reader used to whisper the Gospel story to the exhausted men, trying as he did to ease his own aching hands and shoulders. The officer in charge, however, was heard to say that the Scripture Reader was worth two men in his boat. When they reached the Wady Halfa, the Scripture Reader was immediately drafted to a hospital, where men were pouring in with terrible wounds. He helped with the sick and dying, and as there was no Chaplain, was asked by the Commandant to take the Parade Service. He did so gladly.

A few weeks later his unit moved on, and he insisted, despite the hardships, ongoing with them. By this time he was very short of money, as his pay and allowances from Headquarters had not reached him. When he was down to rock-bottom, a Scottish soldier suddenly said: "Got any money?" "Er, – yes," was the reply (after all he still had one piastre!). "Well take this," said the soldier, holding out some coins. "The Lord told me to give you some money." When asked when it could be repaid, he said: "It's all right, mon, the Lord will see to that." They never met again, but the money lasted till his funds came through.

He did not finish the last stage of the journey up river, for Khartoum fell, and he was posted with his unit back to Cairo. It must have been a sorrow to this Christian man that he could not help his fellow believer, General Gordon.

One encouraging testimony has been preserved from a former Deputy Chaplain General concerning a Sergeant who later became an Army Scripture Reader and did valuable work under God before and during World War I.

The Deputy Chaplain General first met the Sergeant when he was sent out to Malta as a young Chaplain. He found on his arrival that the spade work of a Chaplain's duties had already been done. This Sergeant had been preaching to the troops in camp every Sunday evening, and during the week he had held Bible classes and meetings for Christian fellowship, into which he had gathered the men. On the arrival of the Chaplain the Sergeant had reported to him and had handed over a well organised work which he had been doing so ably single-handed. He became the Chaplain's right-hand man during the rest of their time in Malta. When later in 1898 this Sergeant's regiment was sent to Egypt to take part in Lord Kitchener's Expedition to Khartoum, the Chaplain said:

"I had special opportunities of watching his life and work. During the first six months of the campaign this Sergeant's company was separated from the main body of the British troops and posted some 200 miles away to guard the caravan route across the Bayuda Desert from Korti to Metemmeh. As they were only a few in number, some 120, it had not been thought necessary to send a Chaplain with them, so no man was officially appointed to care for their souls.

"One evening, so the Commanding Officer told me afterwards, while walking round the lines he heard the sound of singing, and found gathered together almost the whole of the men in the camp. They were singing hymns, and he stood back in the darkness and listened. Then the Sergeant preached to them, and the CO said to me afterwards, 'You know, Padre, he knocked spots off most of the parsons I have heard preach. He was right on the nail.'

"After that the CO sent for this Colour Sergeant, and said to him, 'Look here, Colour Sergeant, as long as we are on this job, and isolated from the rest, you are going to be Chaplain in charge of this Company. You will conduct the services and we will all come and hear you preach.' So the parade and voluntary services were conducted by this NCO and when the time came that many of the men were stricken with illness and some of them died, it was the godly Sergeant who pointed them to Jesus Christ, did the last offices at the graveside, and wrote home to their friends in England."

Eternity alone will reveal how many men were brought into the Kingdom through the ministry of this godly NCO. He is typical of the sort of men whom the Council seek to appoint as Scripture Readers today.

On the outbreak of the South African War in 1899 another appeal was launched for providing Scripture Readers, and 12 were sent out. Lord Roberts, the Commander-in-Chief, was especially sympathetic and appreciative of their work. All of them were deployed in fighting areas, and their meetings and services were well attended and accompanied by professions of conversion. A visitor to SASRA Headquarters today can read the autobiography of one of these Readers, Mr W G Ransley. It is deeply moving to see the way the Lord called this reluctant and diffident servant of God, and of how graciously he was encouraged by Dr Edgehill, the Chaplain General. A former Greenjacket, Ransley started his time as a Reader at Aldershot, the same place at which he had received his recruit training. He volunteered to go to South Africa, and served as a Reader throughout that campaign and World War I. He was a simple but articulate man, and an accomplished photographer. His record is well illustrated pictorially as well as with accounts of individual conversations. Ransley reveals himself as a warm patriot with a deep affection for soldiers, a caring heart and a love of a simple, Biblical Gospel. His narrative will interest a modern Reader in that the response which Ransley received in his ministry from unbelievers is not dissimilar to that which prevails today as the same frustrations and encouragements recur. Equally there are records of men, especially those dying and wounded in France, whose gratitude expressed to Ransley will melt the hardest heart. The Association is fortunate to possess such a moving, perceptive and well documented account from a Reader of those times.

During World War I, 64 Scripture Readers were employed simultaneously, of whom as many as 36 were deployed to France and Belgium. One Reader who was with the Suffolk Regiment at the outbreak of war was asked by the Commanding Officer to accompany the battalion to France. He obtained permission from the General Secretary to go, and embarked for France at 0430 hours on 13th August 1914. He had the joy of seeing two men come to faith in Christ during the channel crossing. In the days that followed he worked with the battalion during the memorable retreat from Mons which began on 26th August. During this retreat the Reader ministered to many a wounded man and was the means of saving a sergeant's life. These perilous times also provided exceptional opportunities to point men to Christ. In the same operation there was another Reader who had gone out with a Guards battalion. In describing his experiences later he said:

"The first real prayer meeting took place when we received the terrible news that a retirement was inevitable. A few of us got together, and on our knees we sought the blessing of God on every man from the Commanding Officer down to the Drummer Boy. God heard that prayer and we were wonderfully helped.

"At Landrecies we had a terrible battle, and I think that here we had the first real results of the talks 'by the way'; prayer was answered right back to Mons, and many were brought to a saving knowledge of Christ ... Our band of Christians got so large that I could not be with them all at once, and so they got together in little groups at the close of day just to thank God for His goodness and His mercy. Saved and unsaved joined in those meetings. Many passed away in battle itself; but the most wonderful thing that happened was on the Aisne. Six thousand wounded passed through my hands; all were spoken to who were conscious, and every man of them had prayed to and believed in God; but one man in particular said he had never mentioned God but to blaspheme, never prayed before, but he could pray now.

"Another outstanding incident in my life occurred again on the Aisne, where the men crowded round for a copy of the Word of God until I had none left. I did not know what to do for more. I could not have the meetings often enough for them during those early days of the war. At last in desperation I went to the Adjutant and said, 'I have nothing for the men; they want the Word of God.' He said, 'If you get away from this place you will never get back again, but go away now and pray about it.' When I went back to him at 5 o'clock several papers were ready for me. One from himself and one from the Commanding Officer. They were passes to get me through the lines to 'get the Word of God for the troops'.

"I came back to England and got my supply of Scriptures and went back to the men. They had moved to another place on the La Basse, Bethune Front, but overcoming all difficulties by the Grace of the Lord, I got up to the men in spite of all obstacles and was able to get the Word of God into their hands. The one and only thing the men wanted to know was how to get their sins forgiven, and to know the Lord Jesus Christ as their personal Friend and Saviour."

Lack of space precludes the inclusion of additional testimonies of Readers' ministries during World War I, but there is abundant evidence that the terrible years 1914 to 1918 were exceptionally fruitful for Army Scripture Readers whom the Lord had set apart for these times.

☆　☆　☆　☆　☆

SCRIPTURE READERS IN TIMES OF PEACE

It must be remembered that the first 100 years of the ministry of the Army Scripture Readers took place during the days of Empire. Records show that Readers were placed in almost every station which troopships visited and in most overseas garrisons. In addition to British Dominions and Mediterranean garrisons, Bermuda, Mauritius, Burma and the Channel Islands feature on lists of stations at which Readers were appointed. It is encouraging also to note that the work was supported and encouraged regularly by men who were prominent in military leadership and public life.

About the year 1862 there were five Readers employed amongst troops in Canada, and it is interesting that General David Russell thought so highly of their work that he told the Secretary of the Society that so long as he had a command in Canada, he would free the Society from all charges in his district.

Christian officers in the Punjab and Calcutta formed a branch of the Society in 1872 and deployed 16 Readers in North India. The patrons included the Commander-in-Chief, Lord Napier of Magdala (whose statue, like that of Havelock, is in Trafalgar Square). The list of Vice-Presidents includes the Bishop of Lahore and a Colonel F S Roberts, VC, who was later to become so distinguished as a Field Marshal. Lord Napier is recorded as thanking the headquarters committee in London for sending two Readers to accompany the Abyssinian expedition in 1868. He also testified to the value of Army Scripture Readers' work in most appreciative terms:

> "It has been wisely ruled by the Society that in selecting Scripture Readers, the preference shall be given to men who have been soldiers themselves. No one can more fully appreciate the trials and temptations of soldiers than those who have themselves felt them, have gained a glorious victory over them, and feel a conscientious call to devote themselves to save others ... No one can tell so well when the voice of a friend will be listened to; no one else can have such opportunities of seeing the moment when the path of a young soldier may be turned from evil to good ... I have observed great good from the Scripture Readers' labours; as Commander-in-Chief I sincerely and cordially commend them to the protection of Commanding Officers."

In 1926, permission was obtained for the Army Scripture Reader at Gibraltar to visit the Home and Mediterranean Fleets when they were in harbour, and shortly after this permission had been granted, a second Reader was despatched for a few months to join him. The Admiral issued the following order:

> "Two Army Scripture Readers will visit the whole of the Fleet. Every facility to be given, and the use of Liberty boats."

One Reader commented that this was the best signal since Nelson's! He added:

"There were over 80 ships in the two Fleets, and we visited 48 of their number, amongst which was the largest and newest submarine. Imagine two Army Scripture Readers aboard a ship of the class of *The Emperor of India* and *The Iron Duke* (the late Earl Jellico's Flagship at Jutland with 1,400 men). It was a big thing to attempt, but never have I seen men so eager to hear the Word of God ... The men were so held by the Gospel one night that when the cry rang out, 'A fight on board', they would not leave us, even for that excitement, and over 30 men that night decided to accept Christ. There is no 'hole and corner' religion in the Navy; you have to be one thing or the other. If these men do not stand their ground they have to go through it."

One incident is quoted from the annals of one of the Readers who worked in India:

"On 22nd December, the Senior Chaplain to the Forces called at the Prayer Room and said, 'I am greatly troubled and worried over a Staff Sergeant who is being discharged from hospital today as incurable. I have just left the Medical Officer and they will not have him in hospital any longer owing to his conduct. He has had DT and is now bordering on permanent insanity. He has lost promotion through drink, and if something is not done soon he will be sent home to England, and discharged from the Army without a pension.' He then told me that I was the only man who could do anything for him. He said, 'You have a wide experience in medical work, and I believe if you could get this NCO to your Prayer Room, with other Christian men, and under your care, it might save him from disgrace. It will not be an easy thing to do, especially with Christmas so near at hand, but I shudder to think what will happen if this man is left to do as he wishes. I suppose your Society would not raise any objection to this, would they?' I replied that this was just the Society's work.

"The Staff Sergeant arrived about 3 p.m., helpless, sodden with drink, dirty – in fact, a drunken wreck. He would drink no less than 50 pints of beer in one evening. The greatest thing that had to be fought against was the doctor's report, which said, 'It is strongly recommended that this NCO should not attempt to give up the drink, which would probably prove fatal, but it is recommended that he should lessen the quantity.

"You can imagine how the devil used the first part of this report in the heart of this man, yet by Christmas Day he had been enabled to reduce his drinking from 50 to two pints of beer.

"Today he is a very keen Bible student, and takes a great interest in the meetings, and has been recommended for promotion. One of his superior officers called in the other evening and said, 'I have known Staff Sergeant ... for two years; he was always a drunkard, but today everyone in this Arsenal is watching him, and is amazed at the change in his life. Without doubt he has a lot to thank you for, Mr ...' To which I replied, 'No, sir, I have done nothing. It is the power of the Lord Jesus Christ that has worked this miracle in his life.'"

In an extract from the NCO's letter to the Reader, he said:

"I was in utter despair when I went to the Padre. The doctors could do nothing more for me here. The Padre's prayers did me a lot of good, but only because of his absolute faith in them, and it set me thinking, that if a well-educated, sensible man could ask God for me to be cured, and not only believe that his prayers would be answered, but know without any doubt that they would, then I felt there must be something that I had missed. He then sent me to you, knowing that I should come into contact with other men who were striving to follow the Master, and that was the beginning of the cure.

"When I found that through prayer it was possible actually to talk to Christ, like a personal, living Friend, and to feel His Presence in the room, and to hear strong fervent prayers asking for my sickness to be taken away, and to know that you believed yourself that it was only a matter of time for me to get well, then I began to understand a little. Our little prayer meetings mean a lot to me now, and the Bible has become really interesting and helpful, whereas before it meant nothing."

Later this Staff Sergeant held Bible classes amongst the

men of his own regiment, and proved a splendid witness for Christ.

The last major pre-World War II initiative which the Army Scripture Readers responded to was a request to involve the Royal Air Force in their ministry. Permission was granted by the Air Ministry in 1937 to visit aerodromes. The following appreciative comments were made by the Chaplain-in-Chief of the Royal Air Force after this expansion started:

> "I came into touch with the Army Scripture Readers for the first time while serving as an Army Chaplain in 1905. The Society has recently been given official permission by the Air Ministry, and work at Air Force Stations has begun. I welcome this work in the Air Force, for I know the message taken by the Readers to the men is the Gospel of God's saving power in Jesus Christ, who alone can deliver men from sin's degradation and give them power to set them free to live truly manly lives for their Lord, and for the benefit of their comrades.

It is noteworthy that the first hundred years of witness by the Army Scripture Readers ended with a concern that more Readers should be raised up. No less than 95 had been employed when the work was at its peak in 1883. In 1938 there were 25 full-time and 22 part-time Readers. And yet the Council had cause for encouragement that the Society's ministry had been truly blessed of God, not least by young soldiers being won for Christ in their early weeks of recruit training in the last years before World War II.

The Council recorded that appeals from those in authority for Readers to be provided had had to be turned down because suitable men were not available. Sgt Rudd would surely have endorsed the statement in the centenary magazine that "the hopes and prayers of the Council arise that the importance and blessedness of this work may be brought home so earnestly to the hearts of the Lord's servants, that within the next few years it may be possible to double the number of Readers and so meet the pressing needs which exist in Garrisons, both large and small, at home and abroad."

The way in which the Lord graciously answered that prayer by unexpected means will be described in a later chapter.

CHAPTER 3

THE SOLDIERS' AND AIRMEN'S CHRISTIAN ASSOCIATION

THE FIRST FIFTY YEARS

The official inauguration of The Soldiers' Christian Association (SCA) took place in 1887, but by then there were already groups of Members formed at London, Windsor, Aldershot, Glasgow, Dublin and Cork and these were soon linked together as Branches. The Soldiers' Homes, which ladies like Miss Sandes and Miss Daniell had established readily gave facilities for devotional meetings to be held in their premises, and in India the Prayer Rooms, which had been erected through the energetic work of Mr W B Harrington, became the gathering place of those who were enrolled in the East.

Both at home and in India, membership of the Association spread from centre to centre. It cannot be denied that occasionally steps were taken to hinder the work; yet it is evident that there were instances where the very opposition was so divinely overruled that it led to new Branches being formed.

The foundation laid by the Association in peace was to prove valuable as the work expanded during the exigencies created by the Boer War. At the outbreak of war 400 Branches were in operation. Men who were tramping across the South African battlefields carried with them Bibles and helpful literature, which cheered them in moments of extreme danger. Groups of Christian men would gather together in the evening in some quiet spot to study the Bible, to pray and seek to win their fellow soldiers for Christ. Records of these years indicate that the spiritual hunger of the troops was equal to their physical need of food. At Bloemfontein, for example, a vivid picture of events is described thus:

"Fifty thousand men encamped all about us, seven hundred men down with enteric fever. Our two big tents unable to accommodate the crowds of men professing to accept Christ ... You can form no idea of the interest the men take in our Gospel Services. Some come half an hour before commencing time, to ensure a seat ... Two nights ago the tent was full to overflowing, but the men stood seven deep around the sides outside."

And another Member of the Association involved in the memorable siege during which 600 men professed conversion, records:

"Ross and I started for chapel this morning (Sunday), taking a good number of tracts with us for distribution on our way. These are eagerly taken by the civilians who are here, as well as by soldiers and sailors. Tracts, like everything else these days, are very scarce ... Our horses are getting, like the men, very weak. They are scarcely able to crawl about. When they fall, we have to shoot them, and then carry their bodies to the cooking pot. The men are so thin that their clothes look as though their wearers had got the wrong suits."

The influence of the Association during the Boer War so impressed the Commander-in-Chief, Lord Roberts, that he agreed to become President, an office which he held until his death.

The years of peace leading up to World War I provided further opportunities for the Association's Missioners and Members to win soldiers for Christ and to build them up in faith. It was claimed that no one could be taught as the Association taught its members – the value of regular and informed Bible study, the worth of united meeting for prayer and praise, and the moral strength that was received by the public testimony to personal faith – without being a stronger and better servant of Christ, a more efficient soldier and a more worthy citizen.

These were the routine tasks of the Association. There came, also, demands upon its resources of an exceptional character. The coronation ceremonies for both King Edward VII and King George V involved the bringing to London of troops from all corners of the Empire. Some of these were stationed at the Alexandra Palace in North London, and plans had been completed for work amongst them at that centre, when notice was received suddenly that religious work of any kind was not permissible under the bye-laws of the Palace.

What might have been a bitter disappointment was overruled for good, for within 24 hours permission was received to transfer the operations to Kensington Gardens, where there were 7,000 men, as compared with 3,000 at the Alexandra Palace. In spite of the ban on religious work at the latter centre, it was found possible to distribute there 3,000 specially-bound copies of the New Testament, through the Chaplain General and the chaplain of the camp on behalf of the Association. Notepaper and envelopes were also given to the overseas troops.

In 1911, at the time of the coronation of King George V, facilities were again granted by the authorities to the Association for work amongst the visiting troops. This time the ground allotted was the camp at Wormwood Scrubs, where three cavalry regiments and four batteries of artillery were stationed. Two large marquees were erected and placed at the disposal of the Association. There were some 4,000 men to be cared for, and officers and men alike were full of thanks for the value which these tents, with their atmosphere of home, proved to be to the troops. As far as Members of the Association were concerned, their joy was considerably increased at meeting old friends whom they had known before as followers of Christ.

It was also during the early years of the Association that two activities were initiated which are still prominent in the SASRA calendar. In 1896 the first SCA annual convention was held in Exeter Hall, and attended by about 150 ranks. This proved to be the first "Our Day" convention. As one commentator of the early days of the SCA was to say:

> "There is nothing conventional about such an "Our Day" convention. A freedom of expression is found there, for the soldier is accustomed to many everyday incidents which create in his mind an analogy between his calling as a servant of the King and his higher calling as a follower of the King of Kings."

In 1911 the Association was grateful to the military authorities for not only allowing access to sailors and soldiers participating in the Naval and Military Tournament, but for providing also every facility including tentage. It is still the privilege of SASRA to provide a Rest Room with two resident Scripture Readers at the Royal Tournament,[5] and also at the Edinburgh and Cardiff Tattoos and other similar events. In these rooms a significant number of men and women have come to faith in Christ each year.

A modern reader who has access to accounts of evangelism carried out by SCA workers in the past, cannot but be impressed at their initiative and sense of Divine opportunism. Wherever they saw large formations of troops, they seem to have longed to join them in order to win them for Christ. Among the most fruitful areas of work were the troopships leaving ports to transfer soldiers, who had never left British shores before, to the far corners of the Empire.

It was in these early years of the SCA also that the need was recognised to facilitate members keeping in touch with each other and the Association's activities. Accordingly a periodical magazine entitled *News from the Front* was produced; but when the Association took over the Portsmouth Soldiers' Institute, which already produced a magazine under the title *Ready*, it was this title that was then adopted by SCA and is well known to

5 The Royal Tournament ceased in 19**, see chapter *

SASRA Members and supporters who now receive the magazine periodically.

☆ ☆ ☆ ☆ ☆

WORLD WAR I

When war was declared in August 1914, SCA had 2,000 serving Members and 2,000 Associates. Many of these men were to have their faith in Christ tested in the early months of the war and like their comrades, the Army Scripture Readers, were to find Him entirely faithful in keeping them professionally and spiritually.

In that "contemptible little army" (as the Kaiser called the British Expeditionary Force) were many men who had been brought to faith in Christ in the South African War and the subsequent years of peace. In order to illustrate how these had been taught to value the written Word, let us take a glimpse into a Sergeant's experience during his first days in France.

At about midday on 20th August 1914, the order came that his battery was to be prepared to march to the front at 9.30pm. In his pocket he carried a copy of *Daily Light*. Night had fallen, and he and his battery were waiting for orders. He had already mounted his horse ready to march off. From his pocket he took the little book and turned to the evening portion, and read prayerfully by the light of the great arc lamps which encircled the camp. The appointed passage was Deuteronomy 33:27. "The eternal God is thy refuge, and underneath are the everlasting arms, and He shall thrust out the enemy before thee."

Scoffers may smile at the suggestion that an individual soldier should deliberately appropriate the promise for himself and for his cause. Yet that is what this Sergeant did. It was a promise which he took with him not only through the terrible days of the retreat from Mons, but throughout the whole war. As he stood by his gun before

Mons with the members of his gun detachment, under orders which might well mean death to them all, he urged them to be prepared to meet their God. Four out of the five men that night made the great decision, and continued to bear unfaltering witness until, for three of them, some months after, the end came.

The retreat from Mons is associated in the popular mind with disaster and defeat. It is well, therefore, to lift the curtain on some details which are not usually recounted in official histories or popular war-books. Troops under Field Marshal Sir John French were retreating under conditions which were so exhausting that many of them found it impossible to keep awake. Some fell asleep from sheer exhaustion by the roadside as the army marched steadily onwards.

Even in these extreme conditions soldiers found time to meet and pray. In one unit the SCA members gathered together at midnight, in order that they might read together their Scripture Union portion, and spend a little time in united prayer.

All around them lay comrades who had fallen in battle. Guns of their brigade had been taken by the enemy, and fellow soldiers had been captured as prisoners of war. Yet here were Christian soldiers who found a way of escape from the scenes of carnage. For them, quiet communion with God, and the reading of His Word, meant a renewal of strength and the building up of high resolve.

During the first months of the war, by permission of the military authorities, marquees were erected by the Association in the home camps, and furnished with facilities for letter-writing, reading and rest. Every night a Gospel service was held at which there was always an overflowing audience. When winter came, huts were erected and these gave additional facilities through the provision of rooms for Bible classes and devotional meetings. Here the work of the Association was fostered and increased, thousands of men testifying to the help and blessing received.

Before the time came for demobilisation, there were 19

huts at work. Opportunities came to the Association which were seized gladly. From Commanding Officers there came requests for additional help for their men. From the men themselves came the greatest evidence of all of the blessing and help which the huts were giving, and of lives yielded to the Lord Jesus Christ.

Thousands of young men had rushed to join "Kitchener's Army". For these there existed already a number of societies which catered for the material and social needs of the troops; but The Soldiers' Christian Association Council realised that there was at this time an urgent need for someone to give undivided thought to the spiritual demands which very soon were expressed by those who found themselves face to face with a new set of circumstances, and in danger from unsuspected temptations.

The results were noteworthy. The late Reverend Doctor J Stuart Holden wrote, after a tour of France: "No-one need ever have any doubt as to whether men will come to a hut where there are neither canteen, concerts, cards nor amusements. They not only came to these huts, but entered in such numbers that in almost every centre the crying need was for extension. The difficulty was not to get the men; the difficulty was to find room for all who came and to accommodate them with comfort. Men there were as tired and blasé with amusements as they were weary with the war itself. Such men found the huts of the Soldiers' Christian Association a real home, and many of them, thank God, found there also the Gate of Heaven."

But it was not only those who were already serving the Lord Jesus Christ who were glad to come into these huts. "One night there entered a group of three men", continues Doctor Stuart Holden, "and at once every man in the hut seemed to be thrilled with interest. The ladies in charge were aware that the centre of the little group was a celebrity of some kind, from the stir which his entry caused. In the course of a conversation with him, they discovered that he was a famous pugilist with a world-wide reputation. His companions were also well known

54

boxers. This man, they told the ladies, on one occasion won £2,000 in a few minutes in the ring. He had been matched against an opponent for a 20-round contest, and had knocked out his man at the beginning of the second round.

"The man had never heard of the Crucifixion, or the story of the Prodigal Son. He could not give the name of any book in the Bible. But to him the Gospel story came as a wonderful message. He drank in every word. His mind opened to its beauty like a flower before the sun. He was in the camp for three weeks as a Sergeant-Instructor in Gymnastics. Every day he came to the hut three times for instruction in the Word of God. He left, at the end of his three weeks there, with a sincere and humble faith in the Lord Jesus, and made a bold confession of his faith. He was one of the idols of the men in camp, and the story of his changed heart was told with amazement in every place where he was known."

Others were led to surrender to Christ only when they saw themselves on the very brink of destruction. A Gospel service had been held at one SCA hut, after which the leader, who had to hurry away, was stopped by a big fellow who gripped his hand. "Sir, I've taken Him tonight," declared the man. "I've been waiting for such an opportunity as this ever since the battle of Cambrai. I have a little wife at home who has been praying for a long time that I might become a Christian. Well, I was in a division at Cambrai that was left hanging on without support for four days. Most of my comrades were killed ... but I vowed then that the first chance I got of being converted I would take it. I've done it. I've taken my chance tonight, and He has taken me. I'm just going to write and tell my wife. Oh, how glad she will be!"

Even in the dug-outs were those who met together in Christian fellowship, to pray for some particular comrade whose need was laid on their hearts. A Sergeant wrote later that one of these men was turning out a particularly bright Christian. "He had been definitely laid on my heart for some time. It was after I had had several talks with him that he finally surrendered. I was turning in one night, and just popped my head into the dug-out. 'How is it tonight, George?' I asked. His answer gave me the thrill I was waiting for. 'There is joy in the presence of the angels of God over one sinner that repenteth,' he said. 'Is that you, George?' 'Yes'.

It was not only the notorious evil-livers who were helped to decision. Sometimes there came into touch with one or other of the members of the Association at the Front those who had lived lives which were outwardly correct and almost beyond reproach. One young fellow attended evening service at the invitation of a Sergeant SCA Member. The lad had gone through a terrible experience up the line, but had got back to the base camp unhurt. As he sat in the meeting, he realised how evil he was in the sight of God. He had lived a morally good life, but was aware of the power which indwelling sin had over him. As the meeting progressed, there came to him a great longing for a complete change of heart. Before the close of the gathering he had been led by the Holy Spirit to trust implicitly in the finished work of Christ.

Christian soldiers of this generation knew that if they were to win the respect of their comrades their allegiance to Christ must be open and their manner of life consistent. "Camouflaged religion" was judged to be as despicable as an open denial of belief – and this was believed to be equally true both in times of war and peace. Christians among the "Old Contemptibles" regarded saying prayers under the bedclothes at night, rather than kneeling by one's bedside, as a piece of cowardice which could only bring disgrace upon the religion of Christ. As one of them was to say:

> "A man may as well keep his mouth shut if he never bows his knees before God. If he can't speak with his tongue, he can testify with his knee muscles."

It is appropriate to ask how the Missioners who staffed the SCA huts went about their task of endeavouring to help men come to faith in Christ.

The following account which involves Mr H M Ward, who was one of the SCA Missioners in France, will give some idea of the way God used these men.

Mr Ward had been asked to see that a registered letter was sent to his people at home by a young soldier belonging to a kilted Canadian regiment.

"I'm on draft for the next batch going up to the Front," he said.

"... Are you going up as a Christian?" asked Mr Ward, with that directness which was welcomed by so many of the men to whom the question was put, in those days of danger and coming death.

"No," said the lad, "I haven't the pluck for that. I'm a forlorn hope in that direction. I've tried heaps of times, and failed. I can't stand to my guns when under fire."

Here was a lad, firm of face, square of chin, massive limbed and broad shouldered. Yet he, with an honesty which could only come from one of strong will, confessed his weakness.

"Did you fail when you tried to be a soldier?" asked Mr Ward.

"There is no trying at that game. You enlist, and the Army does the rest," came the reply.

"But if you fail when once you have enlisted, then you are no longer a soldier?"

The soldier smiled at so strange a suggestion.

"Not likely. Once you've signed on, the Army undertakes to lick you into shape. There's no such thing as failing or trying. The thing is done. You're a soldier the moment you join up."

"Before you're trained?"

"You are trained because you are a soldier. They can do nothing with you until you put yourself into their hands. Then you are no longer your own. You put off civvies, and put on the King's uniform, and do as you are told. You are a soldier. The thing is done. That's all. The soldier's life comes afterwards."

"Quite right", answered Mr Ward. "And the same is true of the Christian. You are not a Christian by trying to be one. You put yourself in the hands of Christ. Then you are no longer your own. You belong to Him. He will train you. Once you have accepted His call you are a Christian, just as when you responded to the call of your king you became a soldier. The Christian life comes afterwards. There is nothing in the King's Regulations about trying or failing to become a soldier. And there is nothing in the Bible, from cover to cover, about trying or failing to become a Christian. There is this difference. The Army rejects some who offer themselves. But Christ says, 'Him that cometh to Me I will in no wise cast out.' Now, let me ask you again, will you go up the line as a Christian?"

The lad waited a moment. Then he shook his head. "I should only fail, and that to me would be worse than all."

That night this lad was one of those who came to the SCA meeting in the hut. He stayed behind, and entered the enquiry room. He was not satisfied. When he came out he was still away from God. But he sought out the worker who had so skilfully guided him in the afternoon. To him he unfolded the story of his past failures. He was, he said, an utterly hopeless case. He had been brought up in a very godly home. It had been like a prison to him. There was refinement and comfort, but he could not do as other boys did. He was not allowed to read the books they read, nor go where they went. At last he had broken loose, and his passage was booked to Nova Scotia and, as he thought, to freedom. He had done with family prayers and Bible readings. He felt like a convict loosed from his chain.

Like the prodigal, he rushed wildly into sin. And, like the prodigal, he found the experience far from satisfying. He vowed to do better, and did worse. He tried again, and companions and the lure of the world led him captive. He hated himself and the life he was living. Then came the war, and he jumped at a chance to cut loose from his associations. But he could not cut loose from himself. He enlisted with the determination to follow the advice of his mother, and live the Christian life. But, before a month had passed, he had been defeated over and over again. That night he had become resigned to his lot.

"So you have tried every way but the right one," said Mr Ward. "You have come to yourself, and stopped there. You have never come to Christ!" While these two were talking, there came into the room yet another lad seeking the way of Christ. He had heard Mr Ward's last sentence. "That's just what brought me here, sir," said the newcomer. "I can't understand this 'coming to Christ'. It's troubling me a goodish bit. I've said my prayers many a time, and I've been confirmed and taken Communion. Still I know I'm not right. I went back to my tent after the meeting, but was so miserable that I said to myself, 'I'll go and ask him what he means by it.'"

Mr Ward replied, "I mean that you have a real Saviour. One who died to save you, and who is now living to keep you. He is here, just as really as I am here. He says, 'Come to Me,' just as really as I said, 'Come in,' when you knocked at the door. You came to me for help to understand, and you believed that I would give that help at once. Come to Christ in the same sure faith that He will give you forgiveness and peace."

"But what if I keep falling every time?"

"What does a mother do if her child falls on the way to her?"

"Picks her up quick as lightning," came the reply. "I've watched my wife on her knees many a time, teaching our little Dot to walk. She's caught the little one quicker than she could fall. Do you mean it's like that with the Saviour?"

"Yes, and what is more, He will hold your hand all the time, for you will never be able to walk without Him. And if you withdraw your hand from His, and fall, He will take you in His arms again. Trust Him with yourself and you will know what peace means."

"I will," said the newcomer. As he knelt with Mr Ward, the Canadian, too, knelt with them.

"Lord Jesus, I do come to Thee," prayed the seeker. "I've wanted to for a long time. I've been afraid. I've been looking to myself. Now I am looking to Thee, and I trust Thee with all my heart and soul."

The Canadian, too, prayed. Just a simple cry from his heart, and one which may seem but the call of a child in need of help. Those who have to do with men in their hour of bitterest temptation know that such a prayer as he uttered came from a weary but sincere soul. "Have mercy on me, Lord Jesus ... Forgive and save me ... I come to Thee, my Saviour ... Help me, oh, help me to live straight ..."

The newcomer left the little room after a time of fellowship. "Thank God he came when he did," said the Canadian. "It was the thought of the stretched out arms that showed me the way ... Let me have my letter again, sir, please. I want to let the folks at home know what I've found tonight."

During those war days the workers in the SCA huts prayed earnestly that they might be able to seize every opening that came, and use it for the winning of men for Christ. If a man entered the hut and used the piano for the purpose of reviving memories when a passion for music was the ruling purpose in his life, the player tactfully would be asked to play at the evening evangelistic service, and the workers would unite in prayer that the help thus given might be the means of winning the player to God.

Mr Ward recorded four instances where men of very different types, but all gifted musically, were thus brought into Christian fellowship. One was a player of classical music, the son of a Christian mother. The second was a man with a liking for popular melody, able to attract a crowd of comrades to the piano with selections from catchy song tunes and familiar choruses. Yet a third man was a big Scotsman, who made himself known as a musician by rendering Rachmaninoff's "Prelude". This musician had views of his own about God and religion. "No," he said, "there's too much injustice and sorrow in the world for me to accept a God of love. If I could see any kindly purpose behind it all, anything like the same reason which has made me sometimes punish one of my own children, for instance, it would be different. But the innocent suffer, the very best of us are butchered or blown to pieces, and the man who played for safety and himself, in every department of life, gets the decoration and the cheers of the crowd."

"Did the Lord Jesus Christ play for safety and Himself or get the cheers of the crowd when His life hung in the balance? What He was and is, God is, for they that have seen Him have seen the Father. Could He do wrong? Think of Him. Then ask yourself whether any faith placed in Him can be misplaced."

This man came to play the following Sunday night. He made the piano carry a note of command as he struck up the opening chords of "Stand up, stand up for Jesus". At the close this highlander was the last man to make his way into the enquiry room, seeking, and finding, a faith which overcame the doubts and fears of his earlier comments on a "God of Love".

The war ended on 11th November 1918. The duty staff officer at General Headquarters, who drafted the "ceasefire" signal, was a Christian Colonel who in later years was to become President of SASRA, Lieutenant General Sir William Dobbie.

One of the SCA Missioners has left an account of the reaction to the news of the Armistice in his area of service:

"We had a crowded hut, men reading and writing everywhere, when the communication was handed in from Headquarters. The leader went to the platform: 'Order, boys.' There was a deep hush, then he read out the news, and such a cheer went up that one almost felt like weeping, more than anything else. I looked round on the crowd, fathers who had left home and loved ones, boys with the fear of an unknown future before them – it was a memorable evening.

"For days before we were on the tip-toe of expectation, until 11th November, and then – I don't think I was disappointed at the quiet manner in which the men took the news. I think they were like those of old, 'We were like men that dream'. The crowd seemed like that; some men could not speak of it, and most were wiping their eyes. It seemed too much for them. As evening drew on there were sounds of rejoicing on every hand. The boys were gathered together to be told the news, saluted the flag, the band played 'God save the King' and then came a ringing cheer.

"Our evening meeting was a great time. Organ and piano playing, and a number of men coming out for Christ at the close ...

"We began to wonder what difference the news would make to our Sunday night meeting. Last Sunday, the great Thanksgiving Day all over the camp, we had a glorious day. We prayed that men who might be moved by fear should be few in number compared with those moved by His love. The day began with a crowded hut. In the Bible Class the subject was, 'What shall I render unto the Lord for all His benefits? I will take the cup of Salvation.' At the close hands went up of those who definitely wished to take Christ. At the tea table we had boys from all parts with us, and a crowded prayer meeting afterwards. For the service the hut was crowded with men standing. No seats were vacant, and when we sang 'All people that on earth do dwell', followed by 'Our God is marching on', the effect was unforgettable. The message was on the Word, 'Unto Him who had loved us, and loosed us from our sins.' After this there was a crowd of men who came forward for Christ. His love had conquered. To Him be all the glory for these unforgettable days."

The war proved, as the official records show, that the men who were clear and unmistakable in their testimony for the Lord Jesus Christ were men upon whose skill and courage the Army could rely. Out of the 2,000 who were Members of the Association in August 1914, many were awarded decorations or mentioned in dispatches, and others were promoted for service in the field; while an even greater number laid down their lives in the service of their country.

Many who survived the war were drawn into Christian work outside the services. Missionary societies valued the influence of men who had proved God to be faithful in battle. Here is the message given by a Member of the Association on leave from Quetta, landed in England for the first time for 12 years. The date is May 1920, and the occasion the annual "Our Day" at the Westminster Central Hall.

> "I stand myself a living testimony to the usefulness and power under God of The Soldiers' Christian Association. When I leave the Army, as I may do in a couple of years' time, I shall be ready, thank God, to take up almost any form of Christian work, from the mission field to open air mission work in England. God has blessed me with a faculty for acquiring languages and I want to use that gift in His service. I would like to refer to the missionary aspect of this great work. The soldier who is brought to the knowledge of Jesus Christ in the Army is in the finest ground for missionary training the world has ever known."

That this was no idle word has already been shown in these pages.

☆ ☆ ☆ ☆ ☆

BETWEEN THE WARS

The effect of demobilisation made the work of SCA difficult. Nowhere was this more evident than in India, where the General Secretary of SCA, Mr G J Byrnell, paid a six month visit in 1919. Many of the Regiments which had previously had SCA Branches were now without them, and the Garrison Prayer Rooms were, in many cases, not being used for the purposes for which they had been intended.

The Council of SCA wisely appointed Major F Lee Spratt as the resident Organising Secretary for India. He was a man with excellent knowledge of the country, great zeal and organising ability and well fitted for the task. He and his wife faced a stupendous challenge; many men who could compare the pre- and post-war situations, as indeed Major Lee Spratt could, might have wilted with depression and discouragement. However, his monthly letters home reveal how God honoured His servant, and a steady but significant stream of professions of conversion to Christ accompanied his ministry. The following extract from a letter, sent home by one of these young converts, reveals something of a hunger that was not uncommon, although often unsuspected, even by those who sought to help the British soldier in India between the two wars:

> "We sang several hymns, and the officer gave a short Gospel address, during which there came a great desire into my heart to know about the Lord Jesus. I was afraid to say anything about it to the men present ... The officer explained to me, when I was taken to him, what a blessing it was to be a soldier of Jesus Christ. He took me into a room, and there I knelt down and asked Jesus to forgive all my sins. I had not prayed for years, and at first I could not say a word. Then I just said, 'Lord Jesus, forgive me for my sins. I am sorry for them all.' That was all I could say, but I got up from knees a saved man. Thank God! Since then I have been at every Bible class I could attend, for I was never much acquainted with the Bible and I am anxious to learn as much about it as I can."

In so many of the garrisons, including Agra, Allahabad and Ahmednagar, the ready help and loyal co-operation of the Chaplains of the various denominations added to the joy of the task; while at Lucknow, Major Lee Spratt was assisted at meetings by two old Members of the SCA who had become missionaries.

The work in Germany also gave the Association an opportunity to demonstrate the value of its stand as a spiritual influence. When the huts were opened, many well-meaning friends expressed the belief that it would be necessary to supply cigarettes and tobacco for sale at the canteen counters. Others thought that the Gospel message alone would no longer attract the men. Yet, twelve months after the signing of the Armistice, men were still flocking to the huts and rooms provided by the Association, although neither cigarettes nor tobacco could be purchased there, nor was secular amusement provided from the platforms.

Marshal of the Royal Air Force
The Lord Cameron of Balhousie
President 1977-1985

Major General Sir Laurence New,
CB, CBE
President 1985-1999

General the Lord Dannatt
GCB CBE MC
President, SASRA 1999-
Constable, HM Tower of London

Brig. Gen. H. Biddulph, CB, CMG, DSO
Chairman ASR and SFS 1934-1938
Chairman ASR and SACA 1938-1948

Brig H. A. T. Jarrett-Kerr, CBE, BA
Chairman 1967-1981

Group Captain A. S. Knowles, OBE, AFC
Chairman 1981-

Brigadier W I C Dobbie, OBE
Chairman 1991-

Lt. Col. G. G. S. Clarke, DSO, OBE
General Secretary ASR & SACA and SASRA 1949-1971

Lt. Col. T. A. Dick, MBE
General Secretary 1971-1973

Mr. G. H. Stokes
General Secretary 1973-1981

Lt. Col. K. W. Sear, OBE
General Secretary 1981-1992

Lt. Col. M. Hittchcote, MBE
General Secretary 1992-2003

Sqn Ldr C. R. Woodland
General Secretary 2003-

Fellowship tea at the home of ASR Bob and Kitty White, Singapore

*Part Time Reader ASR George Barker with Junior Soldiers
at Gordon Barracks, Scotland*

ASR Harry Stickings in a Military Hospital

LSR Mrs. J. Derbyshire with group

Scripture Readers at the 1955 Conference

Back Row (left to right): *R. F. C. Westlake (Woolwich),
E. Wigg (N. Aldershot), J. H. Findley (Bordon), J. E. Turner (Blandford),
W. Hitchcock (Portsmouth area).*

Centre Row: *A. Powell (Shrewsbury), C. F. Power (Shoeburyness),
A. Currell (Larkhill), J. Kirk (S. Aldershot), E. Summerfield (Cardington),
E. Frampton (Catterick), A. W. Brockies (Colchester).*

Front Row: *F. Gilbert (Ashford), B. A. E. Hughes (Calne area), J. Swan (Halton),
W. Scott (Locking), J. Duncan (Cosford), W. J. Hall (N. Ireland),
A. J. Boulton (Pucklechurch), H. Stickings (Edinburgh).*

*Two Lady Scripture Readers, Mrs. J. Derbyshire and Miss M. Butterworth
were also present.*

Meanwhile, the work in England was being carried on quietly though with little apparent result. It was decided to conduct a series of evangelistic missions throughout the country and, during the next few years, with the Authorities' permission, the Gospel was taken to 42 garrisons and depots in this way. While the details of the plan to be followed varied as the circumstances demanded, the general outline was the same – barrack-room visitation followed by bright Gospel services.

Colchester was the scene of the first effort. Six experienced workers, going out in pairs, visited every barrack-room in that garrison. This, in itself, was a somewhat formidable task. The reception accorded varied greatly – sometimes hostile, sometimes indifferent, sometimes friendly. And always it was necessary to break down that wall of reserve, which is typically British and which is strangely accentuated in the soldier.

For the first two days the workers were content to leave a written message with every man. On the third day, however, more personal contacts were sought and secured – contacts which, in some cases, resulted in men being won for Christ and lives dedicated to His service. Frequently the workers felt that they had been led, in a wonderful way, to speak to just the men who were conscious of their need and longed for help. Often their visits seemed to be timed by God so that their word might prevent some lad from taking the wrong step he was contemplating.

The composition of the "team" which visited Shorncliffe Camp must have made its appeal to those who noticed it, for it consisted of two ex-Army Chaplains, a Major, two Sergeant-Majors, a young minister and a student. The camp was then occupied by men of the Machine Gun Corps (now the Royal Tank Regiment) and here a very original method was adopted with great success. It was found that the men would not come to the Gospel services, so it was decided to take the Gospel services to the men!

As "Tattoo" (9.30 pm) drew near, and those in barracks were preparing for bed, one of the evangelists would enter a barrack-room and ask if there were any objections to a five-minute service being held. On receiving permission – and only on one occasion was it refused – in would go the portable organ; two verses of a familiar hymn would be followed by a three minute talk, "straight from the shoulder", and an invitation to other meetings. This procedure was followed for a fortnight, and, as a result of the mission, over 30 decisions for Christ were recorded and a branch of the SCA re-established. The Senior Chaplain at Shorncliffe, in a warm letter of thanks to the Secretary, promised to do all that he could to follow up the work thus begun.

Campaigns followed at Aldershot, Glasgow and other stations throughout the kingdom; and, while the apparent results varied, each one demonstrated clearly that the Gospel of Christ is still "the Power of God unto Salvation to every one that believeth". The Chaplains offered a ready co-operation and many expressed their appreciation of the help the missions had been to them in their task of leading men to Christ. Others, hearing of visits elsewhere, sent urgent requests for similar help. There was a challenge in one chaplain's letter: "You will be missing a great opportunity if you do not come quickly. There are many young soldiers here who may yet be won for Christ before they are swept away in the flood of evil around them."

The work was extended to several other towns and camps. In all these centres men were won for God, and in the days that followed messages were received of families honouring Christ, where previously God had not been known, and of men returning home on demobilisation taking up work for Him.

Meanwhile news was received at the office that the men who had been won at Colchester were standing true to their promise of Christian loyalty.

In many centres the Chaplain to the Forces welcomed the Missioners, giving them much help, pointing out men in whom they were particularly interested, indicating what were the greatest difficulties which a young Christian had to meet in that particular garrison, and joining the visitors in prayer meetings and Gospel services. On the evening of the first mission there were four confessions of faith in the Lord Jesus as Saviour. The ground was clearly ready for the effort, as is shown in incident after incident which were reported to the Headquarters of the Association in letters from the Missioners.

☆   ☆   ☆   ☆   ☆

INFLUENCE OF CAPTAIN W H DAWSON

One of the most important of the "Our Day" celebrations was that of 1923. It marked the removal of the offices from Dennison House, Vauxhall Bridge Road, to premises which had been built for the association by Captain W.H. Dawson, late of the Inniskilling Dragoons, one who had spent over 50 years of his life in the service of soldiers. He had been converted to God in 1873, through reading the Memorials of Hedley Vicars. Young Dawson, an adjutant at the time, was completely ignorant of the Way of Salvation when he began to read, and much of the book was "Greek" to him. References to Scripture texts puzzled him. He records that he read a hundred times, one which seemed to have greatly helped Hedley Vicars, without understanding its purport in the slightest degree. The verse was 1 John 1:7: "The blood of Jesus Christ His Son cleanseth us from all sin."

Perplexed beyond bearing, the young man prayed, with a longing which he could not express, that he might have the same experience that had come to the subject of the book he was reading. He fell asleep, wondering what it was he had been asking for, and thinking that perhaps when he awoke next day the idea of his praying at all would have gone out of his mind. But God was very good to this young officer, and next morning Captain Dawson knew that he had passed from death unto life. He at once told his fellow officers. The need for witnessing, which is of paramount importance in the barrack-room, was felt by him to be a matter upon which no questionings were possible. His fellow officers thought he had had some kind of a fit, or seen a vision in a dream. They all agreed that the effect would soon pass off.

Captain Dawson realised that he must separate himself from his old habits. His playing cards were burned. His billiard cues were given away. Tobacco and wine were given up. Race meetings, theatre going, and dancing, lost their attraction. One of the first results of his conversion was the complete change of heart of his soldier servant. Together these two gave up tobacco and alcohol on the same day. At once he began Gospel work among the troops with whom he was associated in Ireland. Quietly, he was able to do away with all swearing by any of the drill staff, on all parades and field days, as well as in Riding School. Captain Dawson was closely associated with Dwight L Moody at the time of the Exeter Hall meetings in which the first steps were taken which resulted in the formation of the Association.

He worked hard for the conversion of men in the ranks, as well as for the souls of his fellow officers. As years went by, he realised the need of a building which would be the property of the Association, and thus it came about that in 1922 he caused plans to be made for the building which was later the Headquarters of the Soldiers' and Airmen's Christian Association – a building which he gave to the Association, together with an endowment fund which relieved the Association of all anxieties arising from the payment of rates and rent.

The Association moved into its new property in Tufton Street, Westminster, 14th April 1923. The official opening and dedication took place on Thursday, 3rd May, when His Royal Highness the Duke of Connaught consented to attend and to declare the building open. Outside the house a Guard of Honour, composed of about 70 Members of the Association, mostly delegates from Woolwich and Aldershot, formed up under Lieutenant McCormack. His

Royal Highness spoke of the pleasure it gave him to be present and to take part in the ceremony. He recalled the days when he and Captain Dawson had been fellow officers in Ireland, and spoke of the Association as "our Association", reminding those present that he had had the privilege and honour of being its Patron for a number of years.

The dedication prayer was offered by Bishop Taylor Smith, Chaplain General to the Forces. In its closing sentences Bishop Taylor Smith asked that the staff who were employed in the new building might make their work their worship and their worship their work, a petition which was afterwards framed and hung in every office and room of the house, as a constant reminder of a great occasion to every member of the staff.

At that "Our Day" celebration, Captain Dawson told the story of the way in which he had been guided in his decision to present the building to the Association. He had not known that several people had been praying for just such a house as he had felt led to build. He had felt that he wanted to give some small token to express his gratitude for 50 years which God had granted to him to serve Him through the Army.

A clergyman known for his eloquent pleading of Christ's cause was the speaker who brought the Annual Meeting to a close. He gave incident after incident which had come to his notice of the help the SCA had been to men who had gone out to France during the war, from his own parish in Lancashire.

After tea the crowning meeting of "Our Day" was held. It was the "Members' Own", and was given over to praise, prayer, and testimony. Between choruses, Members from all parts of the hall rose and told, in simple and moving language, something of their experience as Christians in the barrack-room. Some were newly enlisted in Christ's service, others had years of experience and gladness behind them. But all were full of thankfulness that the Soldiers' Christian Association had ever come into their lives. The gathering concluded with a striking address by

69

one of the members of the Association, who exhorted those present to live in daily fellowship with the Lord.

At a subsequent meeting, there was an effective Bible exposition by the Chairman, followed by a model blackboard meeting, such as was held weekly in the Branches of the Association. One outstanding appeal made by the leader of the blackboard meeting is worth entering in this record. It is one more evidence of the value of the work of the Association:

> "Get hold of the boys in your regiment. Remember that God can save and keep them, when there are so many temptations to pull them down. I was a lad of sixteen when I was invited to an SCA meeting at the Soldiers' Home. I went with a chum, who tried to persuade me to give my heart to God, and I said, 'I'm the worst boy in the Horse Artillery. Everyone knows that.' They sang 'Oh do not let thy Lord depart', and they told me that 'the Blood would cleanse from all sin'. I gave in.
>
> "I made up my mind I would witness by prayer at my bed. If Jesus Christ loved me so much, I must kneel for Him before the fellows. That was how I was saved, and tonight I know that I have had a God who all the way through has never let me down."

The speaker was Lieutenant McCormack who was later to rise to the rank of Brigadier.

☆　☆　☆ ,　☆　☆

WORK IN THE ROYAL AIR FORCE

With the growth and development of the Royal Air Force, the Association received from the Lord a fresh call to service. As a result of the blessings attending this extended ministry, it was thought desirable that some recognition should be given to the Royal Air Force in the title of the Association. Consequently, in the year 1930, it was decided to make the needed change. The movement henceforward was to be known as "The Soldiers' and Airmen's Christian Association".

In harmony with such a change, it was thought desirable also to make a slight change in the Association's badge. Writing of this change, an official of the Association said:

"The original foundation colour of our badge was red, typical of the Blood of Jesus Christ, by which alone salvation is obtained, for without the shedding of blood there is no remission of sins. Red is also the Army colour hence its adoption by The Soldiers' Christian Association. When the Royal Flying Corps was formed, it was part and parcel of the Army, and several SCA members were transferred into it at its formation. But later on it was found necessary to have a separate Air Service, and so the Royal Air Force was formed. This not only necessitated the alteration of the designation from The Soldiers' Christian Association to The Soldiers' and Airmen's Christian Association, but it was found wise to give our Air Force Members a distinctive colour. What could be more appropriate than their own colour – blue? When the new colour badges were made, the opportunity was taken to incorporate the 'A' for 'Airmen's'.

"Not only is blue the colour that the RAF have adopted, but it is also the colour of fidelity. These two colours, red and blue, were used in the drapings of the Tabernacle along with a third colour – purple – which is but a blending of the other two, and is the colour of royalty.

"Instead of having, as heretofore, separate badges for Army and Air Force respectively, the two colours have now been incorporated diagonally across the badge, the upper portion being red, and the lower blue.

"The motto of the SACA is 'Wherefore take unto you … the shield of faith', as will be found inscribed on the scrolls which support the shield found on the cover of the Association's magazine, *Ready*.

"The first two letters in the Greek word 'Christos' constitute a monogram of the name of Christ, which was adopted by the early Christians to denote their faith in Him. Its position in the centre of the badge reminds us that Christ is the central bond of union and source of strength.

"Over the symbol of Christ is placed the Bible with its

radiating rays of light and wisdom, the open page showing one of the petitions in our Lord's matchless prayer. 'That they all may be one' (John 17:21).

"The form of the badge speaks of the conflict in which all Christ's followers were engaged.

"Hence the SACA badge stands for Christ, the previous Blood that He shed, His Fidelity, His Kingly Person, the Bible, and Unity in 'the Good Fight of Faith'."

Shortly after the Association had changed its name, its workers were to rejoice in a notable conversion. A young man who had run away from home joined the newly-formed RAF, giving a false age in order to be accepted. In spite of the careless life in which he indulged, there came to him, while in Iraq, frequent periods of quiet conviction, when conscience was busy, and the memory of his godly home served as a rebuke to his evil ways.

When he returned to England, it was under a deep conviction of sin, and with a soul-hunger for which he could find neither interpretation nor satisfaction. He was accepted to what was at that time No1 Flying School, and threw himself with all his powers into the life of the station. On one occasion a pilot who had completed what is called "Dual Instruction" was given permission to take up his first passenger, and chose this man. For two or three hours the two went on flying and landing, until they realised they were completely lost. A thick mist came up. Presently a hedge loomed up just before them, as they were flying low at 80 miles an hour. The machine went through it, turned a complete somersault, dragged across a road, through another hedge, and finally landed in a ploughed field, upside down, and smashed to pieces.

The two airmen were picked up by an RAF ambulance. One of the men on the ambulance was a SACA Member, who took the opportunity of inviting the injured mechanic to some meetings which were being held in the camp. He accepted, and that night the Great Decision was made. Not long afterwards he received an invitation to attend the Keswick Convention, with results which influenced his whole life. On leaving the Royal Air Force, he eventually accepted an invitation to join the staff of SACA as a Missioner.

Membership in SACA proved to be a tower of strength to these men, because they were encouraged to read their daily portion from the Word of God, and were helped and fortified in the simple meetings for fellowship which were arranged for the Association's Members.

An illustration of what was accomplished is the story of one young mechanic, whose testimony to the living Lord reads like a romance of other days. He had only been a Christian a very few weeks when he was called upon to go up with his pilot, and fly over the Solent. In spite of the fact that every care and precaution is taken in all the flying operations of the RAF, on that occasion something went wrong. Without a moment's warning, the machine swooped down rapidly, and crashed into the sea. By a miracle of Divine Providence, both the pilot and the mechanic were rescued. The fact that the mechanic himself was something of a hero after such a wonderful deliverance provided him with an opportunity which he was swift to use. That same evening he was the centre of an admiring throng who described him as a "lucky fellow".

With perfect simplicity and naturalness the young mechanic, who but a few weeks earlier had surrendered to the Lord Jesus Christ through the ministry of the ASR at Gosport, gave his earnest and unaffected testimony. "I do not think it was luck," he said. "It was God's care of me. Only a few weeks ago He saved me, and today He preserved me. Even if I had not been rescued, all would have been well, for even as the plane was crashing I was conscious of the peace of God which passeth all understanding." Such a testimony has a way of searching the hearts of the unconverted more rapidly than the eloquent sermon.

☆   ☆   ☆   ☆   ☆

A MEMBER'S VIEW

It is perhaps appropriate to end this chapter with an extract from a short article by Captain H S May, who was the Members' Secretary for SASRA for over 20 years. His artless and unsophisticated account captures the spirit of SACA between the wars and, in addition to reflecting the priorities of SACA members of that generation, states the strengths and weaknesses of the Association and reinforces all that has been already stated in this chapter.

"Within one month of my conversion in November 1919 I was introduced to the Soldiers' Christian Association in Rawalpindi. Neither I nor my pal Stewart, converted shortly after me, took kindly to the Branch Secretary because we felt that his military appearance was such a poor advertisement for the Gospel. Appearance and turnout counted in the "old Army", and we in the post war Army believed that Christian soldiers should look, as well as do, their best for Jesus. I began to polish the back of my buttons and badges. Even so, I was only once selected for turnout to be the 'attending man' on guard duty. As I happened to be the NCO marching reliefs, the officer's mistake was pointed out and another man chosen. The late Mr H G Howell, once known as the Senior Army Scripture Reader, told me about a tract distributor whose face would do for a frontispiece for the Book of Lamentations! A member of the public refused the tract with the remark: 'No thanks, mate, I have enough troubles of my own!' It was BQMS Neville who coined the phrase that a good soldier had a clean rifle (meaning impeccable kit and equipment) and a dirty (i.e. well-thumbed) Bible. Whilst aware that the Lord looks upon the heart, understands our thoughts from afar off and knows our inward motives, we believed that, positively, every good SCA Member should read a portion from the Word daily, kneel at his bedside night and morning for witness, and be ready at all times to give the reason of his hope to anyone who asked him. Negatively, we felt that non-Christians (who have a very shrewd idea of what a Christian ought to be) expected us to abstain from smoking, alcohol, gambling and the ballroom. At the same time they hated us for doing so, reminding us that 'there is no harm in it'.

"Our usual SCA gatherings took the form of a Blackboard Meeting and were held in the Sandes Soldiers' Home. No one is absolutely sure whether this most profitable method of Bible Study originated with Sandes or with the Association. These meetings were a tremendous blessing to me in those early days. If we were challenged for our 'best thought' we answered with something from the day's reading. It is a great pity that the Scripture Union daily readings are no longer followed by every SASRA Branch. As a matter of interest, SCA Headquarters in London made a précis of the Daily Notes called 'Daily Rations', which were issued freely with the monthly magazine *Ready*. I regret to say that I made too little use of them. The last part of the Blackboard Meeting was open to all present to say why they chose a particular text. In this way many learned to express themselves who subsequently became 'able ministers of the New Testament'. Those who were unavoidably absent sent in their completed Blackboard Slips together with their comments on the back of the form. This was entered on the 'Muster Roll' and forwarded to Headquarters by the Branch Secretary. Our 'Silver' and 'Golden' Texts were neatly printed on the blackboard and displayed in the main Games and Reading Room. Often we selected Gospel texts containing a challenge. The 'Golden' Text was published in *Ready* and keen interest was shown to see which Branches throughout the Association had chosen our text. Major Molesworth, RE, was among the officers who gave us help and encouragement, also Brigadier General Ewbank (father of Major General Sir Robert Ewbank). On one occasion torrential rain fell just as the General was leaving for his quarters in The Mall. The Lady Superintendent asked me to try and find a gharri (pony-trap) for him. Fortunately I found one, but very foolishly tried to pay the General's fare. No mistake of this kind was ever made again.

"One night I was an innocent eavesdropper and overheard two members of my unit discussing me. Their remarks were far from complimentary, but I shall always remember one of them saying: 'I would not mind if he did not quote the Bible.' I realised at once that I could not hope to hold my own in argument unless I regularly 'acquainted myself with (Divine) orders'. I noted that men like Major Lee Spratt who strengthened our hands in God were men of the Book. They knew their Bibles and how to use them.

"The Soldiers' Christian Association ran Soldiers' Homes at home and overseas. With some exceptions they were not successful enterprises. The biggest problem was to find workers who could cater and cook and at the same time make the spiritual side priority No.1. The SCA huts in France, like so many others in World War I, did a wonderful work for God. The faithful Leader of the SCA hut in Dunkirk sought my soul's welfare as I passed through that camp in 1919. I hope to meet him in heaven. He sowed and others reaped.

"In the summer of 1922 I first met Allen Perry at SCA HQ, Dennison House, Vauxhall Bridge Road. He was a soldier to his very fingertips. Even his parrot could say 'Left right Left right.' Converted as a Trumpeter in the Boer War, he rose to command a battery of Royal Artillery, retiring in the rank of Captain at the end of the War. He was our Assistant Secretary with special care for the Members, while the godly Mr G J Byrnell was responsible for administration, finance, property, publications, etc. These two worthy souls built up the Association when Membership through war casualties and demobilisation was very low indeed.

"The Annual SACA 'Our Day' and the Association's Keswick Convention house parties helped considerably to publicise the work and to recruit prayer-support and funds to maintain it. In a less spectacular way the evangelistic outreach at the Royal Tournament at Olympia and Earl's Court was signally owned and blessed of God. I remember reading a splendid front page article in the *Life of Faith* by a Mr Erswell who was converted as a Private at the Royal Tournament, Olympia. Both Mr Byrnell[1], and Captain Perry[2], were untiring in their efforts to put the Association on the spiritual map of the world. They continually stressed the importance of personal evangelism."

1. Mr Byrnell was converted in a Harrington Prayer Room in India in the mid-1880s. He served as a trooper in the 7th Dragoon Guards and as an Army Scripture Reader with the 10th Hussars in South Africa.
2. Captain Perry won a MC commanding a battery in World War I. He had exceptional ability as an organiser and skill at enlisting the support of the Christian public. He was awarded the MBE for his outstanding contribution to the spiritual welfare of soldiers during his time as Assistant Secretary to the SACA.

CHAPTER 4

AMALGAMATION AND WORLD WAR II

AMALGAMATION

We have already seen how The Army Scripture Readers and Soldiers' Friend Society and The Soldiers' and Airmen's Christian Association came into being, and how God blessed their endeavours during their first 100 years and 50 years of service respectively. A modern reader will inevitably ask why these two Societies were not one and the same, for their purpose and doctrinal foundation were almost identical. The relationship between the two bodies could be described as amicable, with a degree of "trespassing" and duplication in the work. In those quarters where there was suspicion and difficulty, it could be said that this stemmed from difference of approach.

In The Army Scripture Readers and Soldiers' Friend Society, the Reader worked within the Charters laid down by the War Office and Air Ministry. The emphasis was on the Reader's link with Chaplains and, as men came to faith in Christ, the Reader would encourage them to support Garrison Churches and to take part in the more informal local fellowships, often based on the Sandes and Daniell's Soldiers' Homes, or the Mission to Mediterranean Garrisons.

In contrast to this, as it was not primarily concerned with barrack room evangelism, SACA operated without a Charter. It always, however, endeavoured to secure the support and understanding of Commanding Officers and Chaplains. The SACA Missioners were independent, having no official status, the emphasis in their work being on the promotion of Christian Fellowships. Inevitably some of them were tempted, quite wrongly, to regard the Scripture Readers as servants of the Chaplains'

Departments, who were prepared to compromise basic Scriptural truth in order to preserve their appointments. However, the mature Christian men of both Societies were warm-hearted and supportive of one another. The respective governing bodies, whose membership was almost identical, began to pray for amalgamation, and felt led of God to appoint the same General Secretary for both ASR and SACA – Lieutenant Colonel R K A Macaulay, a retired Sapper officer who had been awarded a DSO in World War I.

Towards the end of March 1938, an ASR conference was held which placed the work before the Lord in prayer. It seemed that God directed them to a well-known verse of Scripture: "Enlarge the place of thy tent, and let them stretch forth the curtains of thine habitations: spare not, lengthen thy cords, and strengthen thy stakes" (Isaiah 54:2).

Within a short time the SACA Council unanimously agreed to propose to the ASR Committee that the two Societies should amalgamate. The proposal was accepted without hesitation, and the Societies were legally amalgamated on 29th September 1938, with His Majesty King George VI graciously agreeing to become Patron, and Major General Owen Hay as the President. New Headquarters offices were established at 35 Catherine Place, SW1, and named "Havelock House" after the Christian General who had done so much to win soldiers for Christ. This building had previously housed the Headquarters of the Army Scripture Readers and, like the SACA Headquarters building which was now sold, had been donated generously by Captain W.H. Dawson. A service of dedication was led by the Deputy Chaplain General, Doctor J Lynn, who gave an address which was described as "an inspiration to all", referring to the matchless charter of Christian liberty and faith. Taking 1 Corinthians 3:9 as his text, he said:

"Today we are met to thank God for His goodness to us in the past in our common work among the men in the

Services; to ask for His blessing on this building, which is to house our organisation; and to invite His aid in our labours for the future. We are proud of this handsome house in which we are met, and we realise that it is, above all, His house, to be used for His work. In face of this challenge, then, we sink any differences of outlook or practice which we may have held in time past, and dedicate not only our house, but also ourselves, to Him. 'For we are labourers together with God; ye are God's husbandry, ye are God's building.'

"To be fellow-labourers with God is a privilege, and one which should inspire us to the highest effort; but to be God's building, that is indeed an inheritance divine. No building, no organisation, no planning will be of any avail in this work of ours, unless and until we have given ourselves to Him, so that He may use us as He wishes, without reference to our feelings, or our fortunes. Thus one will lay the foundation, and another will build on it; one will plant and another will water; but on Him, in the last resort, will depend both the harvest, and the house.

"The apostle bids us remember that Jesus Christ is the only foundation. The house built on Him is on a rock, and though the winds blow, the floods come, and beat on our house, it will fall not, because it is founded upon that Rock. Yet on that rock foundation men build their houses of diverse materials. Here there is a wide choice, which may depend upon our birth, education, environment, opportunities; upon our ideas and ideals. Selfishness may produce a house of straw, or even stubble; self-sacrifice a palace of precious stones. But we do well to remember that 'every man's work shall be made manifest, for the day shall declare it, because it shall be revealed by fire, and the fire shall try every man's work of what sort it is'.

"Let us then labour wisely, carefully, prayerfully, whether as individuals, as an Association or as a nation, building upon that foundation which cannot be shaken, a house which will endure for ever, like unto the dwellings in the City of God, prepared from before the beginning of the world. Thus shall we be God's building because we have been built by and for Him."

Three weeks later, on 19th October 1938, the Centenary of The Army Scripture Readers was celebrated jointly with the traditional SACA "Our Day". The first public meeting of the new combined Army Scripture Readers and Soldiers' and Airmen's Christian Association therefore took place in the critical period when Britain approached the Second World War, and Mr Chamberlain made his well-known journey to Munich.

The evening meeting was presided over by the Right Honourable Sir Thomas Inskip, CBE, KC, MP, Minister for Co-Ordination of Defence.

The proceedings opened with the singing of the hymn "We praise Thee, we bless Thee, our Saviour Divine", following which the Chaplain-in-Chief, RAF, the Reverend J R Walkey, led the audience in prayer and the Chaplain General, the Reverend E H Thorold, read the 103rd Psalm.

The following telegram had been sent to His Majesty the King:

"HM THE KING
Buckingham Palace

Members and friends of The Army Scripture Readers and Soldiers' and Airmen's Christian Association, assembled in the Central Hall Westminster on the occasion of their Centenary Meetings and Union, desire to express their humble duty and loyal devotion to your Majesty's person and throne and to Her Majesty the Queen. Wishing your Majesties, the Queen Mother and all the members of the Royal Family God's richest blessing.

H. BIDDULPH
Brigadier General, Chairman"

Lieutenant Colonel Macaulay announced that the following reply had been received from Buckingham Palace:

"The King and Queen sincerely thank the Members and friends of The Army Scripture Readers and Soldiers' and Airmen's Christian Association, assembled on the occasion of their Centenary Meetings and Union, for their loyal assurance of good wishes which their Majesties much appreciate".

The reading of this message was followed by the singing of the National Anthem.

Special thanks were accorded to Sir Thomas Inskip for presiding and identifying himself with the Association. There was also an expression of thanks to the Army and Royal Air Force authorities for enabling Readers and Missioners to go into barracks to spread the Gospel of Christ amongst the men, and to the Chaplains who gave many opportunities that would not otherwise be given.

Colonel Macaulay added that the outstanding event of the past two months, for which much praise to God was due, had been the amalgamation of The Army Scripture Readers and The Soldiers' and Airmen's Christian Association, which had been for 52 years working alongside one another.

The Chairman said he regarded it as a great honour, as well as a pleasure, to be asked to preside at that meeting. They were, he felt sure, all glad to be able to join in prayer and praise to God for the work that had been done by the two Societies, and which it was hoped would be done by them in the future; indeed, it would probably be all the greater because the Societies now worked in intimate relationship. It was impossible to over-estimate the importance of leadership and encouragement which the Chaplain General and the Chaplain-in-Chief of the RAF, and their predecessors, had given to the work of the two Societies. It was good to see them on the platform, and a special welcome would be given to a representative of the corresponding service in the Czechoslovakian Army.

The Reverend Radiskovsky, on hearing his name mentioned as a visitor from Czechoslovakia, stood for a moment, when he received a most sympathetic applause. Obviously the hearts of all present went out in sympathy to him and his fellow-countrymen in that great strain which they had borne with such good order and discipline.

Sir Thomas Inskip noted that the "Our Day" meeting celebrated the history of The Army Scripture Readers, which had existed for 100 years. The British soldier in 1938 was as excellent and brave as of old, but he enjoyed advantages over the men of 100 years ago. The people of the country now took more interest in the Services, and Servicemen were much better educated. Their basic need was, however, still the same: knowledge of and living by the Word of God to attain to the full stature of manhood or womanhood.

There had been celebrated during the past year the fourth Centenary of the publication of the Bible in English. The character of the British people could be attributed to that great event and to that great Book to which they owed the inculcation of the principles of liberty which had marked the history of the race for four hundred years. Some, including Professor Trevelyan, had ascribed to that Book the spirit of adventure and the capacity for enterprise which marked the British race; but, above all, that book gave to the people of the country knowledge of the true doctrine of forgiveness of sin through faith in Christ, which was of inestimable value to the over-burdened soul. Would they not be lacking in their responsibilities, said Sir Thomas, if they did not do everything possible to second and back up the work of the Chaplains of the Army and RAF by giving them the services of the Readers whom the joint organisation would now send out? There would indeed be gaps in our defences if they were not filled with men of God who knew that the greatest blessing in life was to be a Man of God through the teaching of the Bible. For those reasons, he had the greatest possible pleasure in being present, and to help to play a part in what he hoped would be a memorable and happy occasion.

Following the singing of the hymn "A mighty fortress is our God", Brigadier Arthur Smith (Deputy Chairman) delivered an address, and reminded Members and friends that they were gathered together to thank God for the achievements of the past, to realise the opportunities of the present, and to look forward in faith and prayer to God for the future. Looking back over 100 years, there was indeed reason to thank God for all He had enabled the Army Scripture Readers Society to do. It was wonderful to think that throughout all those years there had been those servants of God working in loyal co-operation with the Chaplains, to win men to a saving knowledge of the Lord Jesus, and to build them up in that faith which was based on the Word of God. Looking back over half that time, they also thanked God for the formation of The Soldiers' and Airmen's Christian Association, and for all it had been privileged to do in the binding together of Christian men, who were so grateful to God for the privilege of being allowed to assemble together – officers, warrant officers, non-commissioned officers, men and boys – "all one in Christ Jesus".

They were celebrating the union of two societies, which would now go forward as one in the great task God had allotted to them. The Brigadier picked out from the banner of The Army Scripture Readers Society the word "Scripture", for its work had been in the past, and would be in the future, founded on an absolute belief in the reliability of the Bible from Genesis to Revelation. From the banner of the SACA he picked out the word "Association", because that implied fellowship and was a reminder that they were all one in Jesus. Fellowship was a bond which strengthened, especially fellowship based on the love of God; that was a fellowship which worked because of the power of the Holy Spirit.

He wondered if those present thanked God, as he did, for the remarkable fact that their basis of belief, which so definitely put the Atonement where it should be, and acknowledged God's Word as inspired, had been officially recognised by both the Army Council and the Air Ministry. A wonderful thing. And yet it did not surprise him, because the longer he lived the more he realised how leaders of the Army and the Air Force, and indeed of the Navy, were men who were aware of the need to acknowledge God.

Brigadier Smith paid tribute to two officers on the platform whom God had indeed wonderfully blessed in all the organisation that had been necessary to bring about the union of the two bodies, Colonel Macaulay and

Captain Perry. If there had not been two men prepared to work hand-in-glove and seek the will of God, it would have been impossible to achieve such a satisfactory union. Tribute had already been paid to the Chaplains without whose goodwill, sympathy, and help, it would not be possible to carry on the work with so little friction. In taking stock of the present, all rejoiced that God had brought about the union for which some had been praying and working for years past.

Turning to the future, the Brigadier reminded the audience that the Fighting Forces of the British Empire represented the largest Missionary Society in the world. Every man who went abroad, and indeed those who remained at home in the Forces, were missionaries for God or the Devil. Oh, that more might be missionaries for God. There was in the future much land yet to be possessed, and as a thought for that period the speaker reminded his audience of the human story to be found in 2 Chronicles, chapter 25. Amaziah had collected a great army, hiring also men of valour out of Israel for a hundred talents of silver. But there came a man of God to him saying, "O king, let not the army of Israel go with thee." Amaziah's reaction was typical. He thought of his pocket – what was he to do about the hundred talents of silver he had spent? Were not we all apt to think of earthly things, with the result that the spiritual vision and outlook became blurred? The messenger from God had replied to Amaziah, and one could imagine his kindly smile as he said it: "The Lord is able to give thee much more than this." Those were the words to keep in mind when pondering over what God had already done to help in the past, and when looking forward to the future.

Naturally, of course, the blessings God would give in the future depended upon the measure of faith shown in Him. With a clear grasp of what He wanted them to do, their faith would grow stronger, and the closer they got to Him the greater would be the mighty works God would do for them. God grant continuance of faith and a prayerful spirit, and the belief that the Lord was able to do much more in the future than He had done in the past.

After two Scripture Readers and two former SACA Missioners had given accounts of their work for Christ, the Reverend Colin Kerr gave a moving and penetrating address, expounding Matthew 14:35-36: "And when the men of that place had knowledge of Him, they sent out into all that country round about, and brought unto Him all that were diseased: and besought Him that they might only touch the hem of His garment: and as many as touched were made perfectly whole."

The meeting closed with the singing of the Doxology and the Chaplain General, the Reverend E H Thorold, pronouncing the Benediction.

The prayers of mature Christian men had been answered, but good judgement and sensitivity would clearly be needed for the coming years. Missioners had never before been under the direction of Chaplains, and Readers now had responsibility for Members of the new Association. The Scripture Readers (as all full-time employees of the Association now in contact with troops were called) were expected to link Members up, to encourage and teach them, as well as training them in evangelism and leadership. All Readers were expected to be able to run a meeting.

Qualification for Membership was limited to three things: a genuine conversion to Christ, evidence of a New Life in Christ and a desire to witness for Christ.

In July 1939, the first combined Keswick House party was held, and was a time of real blessing and spiritual uplift. On 26th August, when the outbreak of war seemed imminent and it appeared that the Association would be called upon to inaugurate a tremendous scheme for expansion, the General Secretary, Lieutenant Colonel R K A Macaulay, was called up from Reserve; and soon after, the Secretary, Captain Allen Perry, was taken ill and had to be removed to hospital. This double breach, occurring in a time of national emergency, was a calamity of the first order, and the Association owed a debt of gratitude to Lieutenant Colonel D C D Munro, who undertook to fill the dual office for the time being. Major General William Dobbie also rendered valuable service by acting as Honorary Director for some months, before taking up his duties as Governor of Malta.

During this period the first hut for Servicemen was erected and opened. In January 1940, the Council appointed Major W Mainwaring-Burton as Honorary General Secretary, and the work began to expand rapidly as more and more men entered the ranks of His Majesty's Services, and many new Readers were appointed to meet the increasing need. Throughout the war period, as always, our Readers were greatly helped in their work, both at home and abroad, by the sympathetic co-operation of Army and Air Ministry Chaplains, who, whether as members of the Council or in their contacts with the Readers, gave them every possible encouragement.

☆　☆　☆　☆　☆

WORLD WAR II – EARLY DAYS

The record of a century of spiritual endeavour among the men of the Services has no period that can compare with the activity of the years 1939-1945, for never before had war been waged to such a wide extent. At the outbreak of hostilities, 65 Readers were at work; by the beginning of 1940, 20 had been added to that number, six of whom were awaiting orders to proceed to France, one of these later testifying that his work among the troops in that country was the happiest and most fruitful he had ever known. By the middle of 1940, the number of Readers had increased to 132, and by the end of the year there were 150, the peak number being 183, apart from Lady Scripture Readers for work among ATS and WAAF, for whom the Charter had been extended in 1940.

Readers immediately recognised that the new conditions brought heavier responsibility and widened opportunity, and they readily accepted the one and seized the other. Let one example speak for the rest.

On that memorable Sunday, 3rd September 1939, when so many listened breathlessly to the radio, and at 11.15 am heard the Prime Minister's declaration that Britain was at war with Germany, the Seaforth Highlanders were in Maryhill Barracks. All the men were confined to barracks and great excitement prevailed. The Reader stationed at Glasgow obtained permission to go in and conduct community singing. About 200 men gathered, including a few officers and many NCOs. The Reader soon had them singing choruses and well-known hymns of their own choosing. Realising the tragic possibilities ahead for the men into whose faces he looked, he then asked them if they would like him to give a brief talk from the Word of God. Subdued by the solemnity of that hour, they expressed their readiness to listen, and from John 15:13 the message of Redeeming Love was proclaimed. At the close three young men came boldly out and made a profession of faith in Jesus Christ. In barracks elsewhere there were similar scenes, and many professions of faith in Christ.

Just before war broke out the Militia Scheme was introduced, and to meet the need thus created an offer of a gift was received from Mr J Laing, to be devoted to the erection of huts.

The offer was gratefully accepted by the Council on 4th September, and the first hut was erected in the centre of camp at Blandford, Dorset. It was dedicated by the Assistant Chaplain General, the Reverend W G Hughes, on 5th December 1939, in the presence of the Officer Commanding, the Garrison staff, Church of England and Nonconformist Chaplains, the donor and others.

The hut was in three sections. The largest, which could accommodate 350, was used for meetings, the smallest for reading, writing and private talks, the third section providing living quarters for the workers.

One of the earliest moves of the Council was to appoint Messrs Robert Laidlaw and Montague Goodman as Honorary Field Directors, the former remaining in this country in order to devote his energies to the work of the Association, instead of returning to his home in New Zealand, from whence he had come on holiday. To meet the war emergency, the most pressing need appeared to be the recruitment of more Scripture Readers and establishment of huts and rest rooms to provide physical, mental and spiritual refreshment for the men who were pouring into the Armed Services. In order to acquaint the Christian public of this project, the Field Directors toured England, Scotland and Ulster. Their appeal met with a ready response by both prayer and financial support.

Before the war, Scripture Readers had been doing good work among airmen in a tent near the Air Base at St Athan, 16 miles from Cardiff. At the commencement of hostilities this had to cease, but the desire to meet the greatly increasing needs continued, and as the result of an appeal made by the Field Directors at a crowded meeting in the Minster Gospel Hall, Cardiff, a local committee was formed, funds were raised, land obtained free for the duration of the war from the local Council, and a large, empty wooden structure in Cardiff was bought. It was removed and re-erected and furnished at St Athan. These premises were opened on 25th June 1940 by Brigadier General H. Biddulph, the Chairman of the Council, and Messrs Goodman and Laidlaw remained for 10 days for special evangelistic meetings. The place became immediately popular with the men at the Air Base, and later, when women of the WAAF were posted to St Athan, another wooden building was added for their special use. Thousands of men and women were thus helped and brought under the sound of the Gospel, many of whom were definitely won for Christ.

Envisaging the needs of the men of the British Expeditionary Force, interested friends in Ulster launched a £1,000 appeal for the provision of a hut to be erected in France. More than twice the target figure was realised, but circumstances, then unforeseen, prevented its reaching the intended destination.

For the purpose of selecting suitable sites for huts and

localities for Rest Rooms, the Field Directors made a reconnaissance of the British sector in Northern France in the early months of 1940. Two Rest Rooms were subsequently opened at Nantes and St Nazaire, where the efforts of Readers were richly blessed. There they had a great opportunity among men who, being some of the first to be drafted from England, were feeling homesick and lonely, and were therefore in receptive mood. The first soul to be won at St Nazaire was a young soldier who, when a Gospel address had been given, asked for a personal talk. He said his wife was a Christian, and he was wondering whether he would ever see her again. He was under conviction and wanted to get right with God. After having the Way of Salvation more fully explained to him, he accepted Christ as his Saviour, and asked the Reader to write to his wife, telling her the good news. This he willingly did and some weeks later received a letter from her, expressing her joy in hearing of her husband's conversion.

Thenceforward it became the policy of the Council of the Association to invest money in men rather than buildings, and, in view of the fluctuating movement of troops, instead of erecting huts, to use Rest Rooms, which were usually either hired or loaned free of rent and could be given up at short notice.

Altogether 35 Rest rooms were opened in various parts of this country, each of which had to be equipped and furnished, a licence for the sale of refreshments obtained, and a staff of voluntary workers organised. To that vast army of helpers who, despite black-out, raids and other difficulties and dangers, spent long evenings, in many cases after a tiring day at business or home duties, the gratitude of the men and women of the Services was frequently expressed. An airman, who regularly travelled 18 miles to attend the weekly Blackboard Meeting at the Rest Room in Edinburgh, wrote later from North Africa, "I look back with pleasure to those happy Friday evenings. What fellowship was ours in Christ! I also look back with pleasure to the good teas Mrs K. gave me on Sundays.

What would I not give for a cup of her tea now!"

Reference has been made to the fund opened in Ulster for the erection of a hut in France. The generous response to that appeal made possible the opening, on 11th December 1940, of a Rest Room for soldiers and airmen in Ballymena, County Antrim. Furniture, given or loaned by friends, included a piano and wireless set, and at the canteen in was possible to obtain a cup of tea with a sandwich or buttered scone for twopence, and quite a substantial meal cost only a few pence more. The object of this side of the work here, as in all other Rest Rooms, was to attract Servicemen to a centre of Christian influence, by ministering to their physical needs. Each evening closed with an Epilogue, which included a brief, direct Gospel address, and many who had almost nightly availed themselves of the amenities and fellowship, spoke appreciatively, and even with emotion, when about to leave the town, of the comfort and strength they had found there.

The work in Ulster was most encouraging. A second Rest Room was opened in North Belfast, where many were definitely converted. When the troops left the district, another Rest Room was provided at Banbridge, which was formally opened on 30th September 1943, and there the work continued for as long as there was a need for it.

Sunday, 14th December 1941, was a red-letter day in Belfast, when a military service and rally, held in the large Assembly Hall, was attended by over 1,500 people, including officers and men of HM Forces and nine Scripture Readers. At that meeting a soldier from Ballymena was converted, and an Officers' Christian Union meeting was started.

Among the most successful Rest Rooms in this country was that at Taunton, which functioned from August 1940 to the end of the war. Here the Reader in charge had the unique opportunity of reaching men of most Regiments in the British Army, as well as men of the American Army and Navy, at the large convalescent camp nearby. The premises, situated in an excellent position in the very centre of the town, was selected by Mr Montague Goodman. The entrance from the street opened into the largest room, in which was the canteen. Behind this were a smaller room and the domestic offices. The reading and writing room on the first floor was furnished with comfortable easy chairs, and adjoining it were two rooms, one of which was the Reader's office. The other was later furnished for the use of women in the Auxiliary Services.

These Rooms were kept open nightly until 10 p.m., the workers agreeing that if the public house next door could continue until that hour for profit, they could do the same for greater profit. Hundreds of letters, every one of which was personally answered by the Reader, testified to the lasting help and blessing of the Sunday evening services, and scarcely a Sunday passed without some men finding the Saviour. One, writing after he had left Taunton, expressed his gratitude for "what you did to help me to find Christ," and went on to say that it was his aim to win others for Him. A gunner, who was lying drunk in the gutter the night before he was converted, became a living witness to the saving and keeping power of Christ.

Possessing unique gifts which God had used, the Taunton Reader was chosen in 1944 to join a team of workers who were appointed for work overseas. To him it was a direct call from God, and although this was also recognised by the voluntary staff and by those who frequented the Rest Rooms, his departure was a source of very real sorrow. A private who heard about it after leaving Taunton, wrote to the Reader expressing the hope that "your mission overseas will meet with equal success. With God's help it will. I shall pray for your safety."

Thus, as the war became worldwide, the Association reviewed the disposition of its workers, seeking to place them where they could render maximum service among the men and women of the Armed forces.

☆　☆　☆　☆　☆

THE BRITISH EXPEDITIONARY FORCE

As in the earlier conflict of 1914-1918, Army Scripture Readers followed the troops into the various theatres of war, and there, sharing with soldiers and airmen the dangers and discomforts, the toil and the turmoil, a service of vital importance was performed. A number were with the men of the British Expeditionary Force in France. Despite black-out and bitterly cold weather – the winter of 1939-1940 was the worst France had experienced for 80 years – they plunged immediately into work. They were at the dockside to meet troops as they disembarked. They were greatly helped by the French YMCA, who assisted in tracing men in their scattered billets and allowed the use of a room for meeting. Rarely have men been more grateful for the Reader than in those days. For Militiamen it was their first taste of active service.

Readers travelled many miles by train and on foot to reach men with the Gospel, and wherever they met them, in the train, on the road, in hospital, office, tent, hut, billet, or even in an estaminet, they listened attentively to the message and gratefully received a Gospel or Testament.

Their presence in France was also greatly appreciated by Army officers. A Major, after enquiring as to the exact nature of their work and learning that they were there primarily to help the men spiritually, expressed his profound pleasure and said, "If I get any hard cases, I will let you deal with them." They were not immediately rewarded with visible results. For a fortnight they prepared the ground, sowed the good seed and watered it by their prayers, and then one man surrendered to the Lord, the first fruits of a bountiful harvest.

Readers were on the happiest terms with Army Chaplains, at one period taking part on alternate Sundays with the United Board Chaplain in the evening service. Paying tribute to their selfless labours in France, the Assistant Chaplain General, Headquarters, Lines of

Communication, wrote with reference to Mr Buchan, who was in charge of the Readers with the BEF:

> "His appointment was a wise one, for, though a veteran, he was tireless in touring the vast areas behind the lines, sensing their needs, suggesting where the Readers might be best used, and giving his colleagues the benefit of his wide experience and advising them how to tackle local problems and difficulties.
>
> "Nor did the other Readers spare themselves. Evidence was always to hand from Officers commanding Districts, and from Chaplains of all denominations, of what it meant to the men in the great camps to have the Scripture Readers with them for quiet reading of God's Word and for worship."

Many lonely Christians were thus helped to bear the trials of separation and to confess Christ before their comrades; backsliders were restored and many unsaved brought to a knowledge of the Truth. Numbers of conversions took place among men who were *en route* for the battle line; for some it was their last opportunity of hearing the Gospel before being ushered into Eternity.

The men were loud in their praises of the Rest Rooms, which provided the only comfort they knew in those days. "The first bit of home I've had since I came out," was the grateful comment of a young fellow as he sank into one of the easy chairs. Games and literature were supplied by Christian organisations and friends at home, who also supported the work with their prayers. At one centre a French lady sent choice flowers every week to give an additional touch of cheerfulness.

But this fruitful service was of short duration. With the evacuation of the BEF it ceased. At that time there were 12 Readers in France, working in pairs. The days following the capitulation were anxious ones, when extreme concern was felt for the safety of the workers, and in specially convened prayer meetings they were commended to God's care.

The first indication of the amazing answers granted to those prayers came when, on one memorable afternoon, five Readers walked into the Headquarters office of the Association, the telegram sent to announce their safe arrival in this country having miscarried. They had a remarkable story of deliverance to tell. On receiving the order to evacuate, their thoughts turned to their colleagues in the forward areas, but their endeavours to make contact with them were without results. All means of communication had been cut; the roads were impassable owing to refugee congestion, and trains were not running to schedule. It was, therefore, a matter of utter reliance upon God for their safety. The five Readers were themselves bombed before embarking, and again during the voyage to England, but the boat escaped serious damage and in the mercy of God they arrived safely in port.

In the letter quoted above, the ACG gave the following description of their departure:

"I remember a broiling hot afternoon towards the end of May, looking from my office window at Headquarters, and seeing the Readers from Rouen struggling along, weighed down under the burden of what kit they had been able to save, but still with a cheery greeting for the tired men they passed. I felt then that men such as these were indeed doing the work they had gone forth to do and doing it in the spirit of their Master.

"I was as sorry to have to collect them and put them on board at St. Nazaire, as they themselves were to go. I found them sitting very quiet in the room they had furnished there, and which had meant so much to them and to the many who used it. It was the only time I saw the Readers downcast. But I rejoice that they all returned to the United Kingdom in safety and hope that now at home, and again when the BEF returns overseas, they will be there to continue their witness for Christ amongst our soldiers and airmen, who must live and serve the better for knowing Whose they are and Whom they serve."

Two days later news was received of the safe return of the remainder of the Readers from France. They also were able to tell of God's wonderful intervention on their behalf. Some were contemplating a few days' leave before moving to another station further up the line, and had booked their passage from Dieppe. But when they reached Paris they learned that the Germans had broken through and were in possession of Dieppe. They then boarded a train to Le Havre, but on arrival there were told that no boats were running to England. However, in answer to prayer, the Lord wonderfully undertook for them and they reached Southampton without mishap.

A few Readers came through Dunkirk, and amid those harrowing scenes on the beaches, where men in their extremity were everywhere calling upon God for forgiveness and deliverance, their opportunities for presenting Christ as the Saviour were so vast that they were unable adequately to cope with them. Nevertheless, regardless of personal safety, and with unflagging zeal, they moved amongst that distracted throng, dispensing the only message that could bring comfort and preserve sanity, and during the weary hours of waiting for physical deliverance, scores experienced the Lord's power to liberate from the prison-house of sin.

Many more who were rescued while yet unconverted were successfully helped by Readers in this country. The wounded were visited in hospital; others, exhausted after days and nights of weary marching while enemy bombs rained down from the skies, found their way into Rest rooms. All had prayed for their lives to be spared, and prepared by the Spirit of God in the fearful ordeal through which they had passed, they were as grain, waiting only for the sickle.

Among these was an atheist who, having found himself in utter helplessness on the beach at Dunkirk, realised that he had neither a foundation for life nor security for eternity. In agony of soul he cried to God for deliverance and was heard. He later arrived at a Reader's hut, firmly convinced as to the existence of God, but professing inability to believe in the Incarnation or the substitutionary nature of Christ's death. He was given a copy of St. John's Gospel and urged to read it prayerfully. This he promised to do, and when he returned the next night his face was radiant, for in the sacred record he had come face to face with "the Lamb of God which taketh away the sin of the world", and at the foot of His Cross had found pardon and peace.

☆ ☆ ☆ ☆ ☆

OUTSIDE EUROPE

After the evacuation from France, it soon became evident that the war's centre of gravity was moving to the Mediterranean and Middle East. Accordingly, Readers, as they were available and as the need arose, were posted to strategic positions in these areas. Gibraltar and Malta each had one and diaries reveal what busy, intense and fruitful ministries they had; another, lent by the Sudan Interior Mission, found a needy mission field among his own countrymen on war service in the Sudan, and others were distributed among the troops in Egypt, North Africa, Palestine, Syria, Iran and Iraq, under the supervision of Mr J S St Clair. Their work began from the moment they stepped on board the troopship, where, on the crowded mess decks, they had a glorious opportunity to present the Gospel of our Lord Jesus Christ.

Each week through the voyage several meetings were held, and God richly blessed the witness. Two Readers on one ship began meetings with five men, but before long 20 were trying to squeeze themselves into a two-berth cabin. In tropical heat they were warm gatherings in more senses than one, and prayer was offered that the use of a larger room might be granted. When the "dry" canteen was placed at their disposal, the number often rose to 60 and was never less than 40, and at these meetings the unconverted were brought to Christ, backsliders were restored and Christians strengthened.

ASR Frank and LSR Vera Crofts, 1952-1981

ASR Gerald and LSR Ivy McClelland, 1946-1985

ASR Ted and LSR Lily Frampton, 1954-1979

ASR Derek and Mrs. Heather Brooks recieving Commander-in-Chief's Commendation.

Captain and Mrs. H. S. May – "Two Firsts"
First Members' Secretary SASRA
First Lady Scripture Reader into action

Soldiers Rest Room in Europe, 1939-1945

Scripture Reader Frank Crofts leading the Children's Holiday Club, Aldershot

ASR Billy Hall and SASRA group

ASR W. Scott (Scotty) and SASRA group

ASR Bill McCully talks to the men. Thirty-seven turned to Christ this year.

"Our Day" Westminter Central Hall

The Platform Party

Testimony Time

SASRA House Parties

Keswick 1965

Filey 1966

A blackboard meeting in progress with ASR Alf Brockies

ASR Ivor Sherwood making contact with men on the Tank Park

On Sunday evenings Gospel services were conducted on one of the decks, where between 500 and 600 men would gather to sing well-known hymns and hear the Gospel. On the last Sunday of this voyage the service was held in the recreation room, which was crowded to capacity. The chairman was the Church of England Chaplain; the Church of Scotland Chaplain read the lesson and the Scripture Reader spoke from the text "Christ Jesus came into the world to save sinners". At the close between 20 and 30 men professed conversion, and two backsliders returned to the Lord.

It was a remarkable voyage from every point of view. The sea was calm all the way, and nothing occurred to dissipate the effect of the Readers' ministry. Moreover, encouraging though the known results undoubtedly were, they did not represent all that took place, for later, in Syria and Egypt, Readers met again men who had sailed with them and who confessed that as a direct consequence of hearing their testimony, they had since decided for Christ.

The work in the Middle East made very great demands upon Readers. There they were more closely identified with the troops in their dangers, following them in the desert warfare and sharing with them all its dangers and discomforts. One writing from a forward area in Libya said, "The desert just now is anything but a desirable place to dwell in; the cold, the sand storms and the debris of war make desolation more desolate." Entering Tobruk just as British tanks were drawing out, jubilant after their victorious advance, the Reader was able to talk and pray with small groups, men turning aside, even in the rush of operations, to hear the Word of God. At a Soldiers' Home in Khartoum, Readers had the help of Lieutenant D Stokes, formerly of the Bible Churchmen's Missionary Society in Abyssinia. Here a sports room was equipped and a weekly blackboard meeting started. Each evening free teas were provided, followed by a Gospel meeting, to which numbers of men were able to look back as the birthplace of their souls.

In the early months of this campaign, the Vice-Chairman of the Association, Lieutenant General Sir Arthur Smith, who was Chief of Staff to the Commander-in-Chief, Middle East, realised the absolute necessity of providing Readers with some form of transport, and at Headquarters a cable was received asking for a public appeal to be made for £150 for the purchase of a lorry for the exclusive use of Scripture Readers in the desert. After hearing the cable repeated over the telephone, the whole amount was donated by a lady who occasionally helped in the office of the deputation staff. Carefully designed to ensure its being desert-worthy, it gave magnificent service until it fell to pieces and was replaced by the military authorities.

A Reader who travelled many hundreds of miles on the lorry, made history with his accordion. Setting the Gospel to music, he drew men around him whenever circumstances permitted, and hundreds sang to its accompaniment in all parts of the desert, and in many strange meeting places, including the underground ward of a casualty clearing station, caves, dug-outs, and in the weekly tent meetings for Kaffir soldiers, where a native sergeant who could speak English acted as interpreter.

Often meetings had the more sinister accompaniment of not very distant guns. After losing his way in the Libyan Desert, a Reader arrived at a place which bore the marks of several months of siege. During a brief stay he was entertained by the Chaplain, who was housed in a building that threatened to collapse at any moment. He was invited to preach in the "church", a disused cinema, where, above the roar of AA guns, he shouted the message of salvation to a "full house", made solemn and attentive by the fact that death was all the while hovering overhead.

A Reader accompanied the Force sent from the Middle East to Crete, where, amid the trials and perils of that disastrous campaign, he exhibited the same courage and endurance as the troops. Visiting an anti-aircraft position just before enemy parachutists dropped, he was cut off from his base some 12 miles away. With the men he went into action against enemy aircraft and helped to render first aid to the wounded. The next day, the Germans having discovered their position, they were straddled by 54 bombs, but mercifully there were no casualties, although the Reader was buried in dirt. Later returning to his base at Canea, he found that most of the town had been destroyed, and under heavy bombardment from the air he worked indefatigably in the theatre of the hospital, with remarkable skill assisting the surgeons in the performance of operations. In this part of the island he also visited German wounded, distributing among them tracts in their own tongue he had brought from Palestine.

When, owing to constant bombing, the position became untenable, most of the wounded were evacuated, the Reader being placed in charge of one party. During the journey of over 40 miles they were frequently bombed and machine-gunned, the Reader at one time living for two days under a culvert in the road. When it became possible to make a break for the beach, with strength almost spent, he helped to carry the wounded on board the waiting boat, where, as soon as all were safely embarked, he sank, exhausted, and was soon asleep. About 100 miles out they were again attacked by enemy aircraft, whose bombs brought death to 12 men, after which, without further incident, the rest arrived safely at Alexandria. Subsequently this Reader, who so valiantly served his Lord, was killed by enemy action.

Meanwhile, the Reader with the accordion continued to accompany the advancing troops in North Africa. In order to attract a crowd he played chorus tunes whenever it was convenient, and usually it was not long before a large company had gathered to whom the message was given. At that time events were moving so swiftly in the Middle East that news from Readers was out of date before it reached Headquarters at home. One of the vivid stories which eventually came to light was that of a Reader's 900 mile ride across the desert on the back of a water lorry, from the driver of which he begged a lift when his car broke down midway. Uncomfortable as this means of transport must have been, he stuck to it, determined at all costs to maintain contact with the famous Eighth Army, to which he was attached.

It was Christmastime when the victorious Eighth Army crossed the Mediterranean to Sicily and Italy, and the Reader with the accordion and three others went with them. Two travelled by troopship, and on Christmas Eve they held a service on board. To the accompaniment of the accordion, carols were sung from sheets typed by the Chief Wireless Operator. The majority of the ship's personnel were present, the Chief Engineer read the lesson and a Reader gave a talk on the need for forgiveness and faith in the Lord Jesus Christ. Within a few hours of their arrival in Italy, the Readers linked up, and while waiting for final directions from the Assistant Chaplain General, North Africa, they were posted to a Transit Camp, where the Lord set His seal to their ministry in conversions. Later all were moved up to more forward areas, where they were again in the thick of operations.

With resourcefulness and originality they sought to adapt their methods to circumstances, that the greatest possible number of men might be reached. Among those were the placing of suitable verses of Scripture in prominent places along the famous Route 6, that thousands might be reminded of the Word of God before going into action, and giving five minute talks to men on gun sites, and to sappers engaged in making roads and bridges. They were with the men before Cassino, and in a large camp north of Naples, where men returning home waited for their passage and others passed through on their way to join their units in the front line, one of the most far-reaching ministries of the war was exercised.

Reference to the work at Gibraltar was made in an earlier chapter. Malta had two Readers, who ministered to the men who so heroically defended this vital Mediterranean post. While engaging in this hazardous task, they were encouraged and strengthened by the sympathy and Christian witness of Lieutenant General Sir William Dobbie, the Governor, whose care for the spiritual welfare of the troops was inspiring and active throughout his term of service.

Everywhere the Readers found a ready ear for the Gospel. While speaking one day to a number of men, another man approached and joined the group, and was delighted to find that he was listening to an Army Scripture Reader, having just previously received a letter in which the hope was expressed that he might be brought into touch with one of these devoted servants of Jesus Christ.

At Sarafand in Palestine, through the generosity of a lady in Scotland who wished to remain anonymous, Mr St Clair was enabled to erect a hut, which proved to be a veritable spiritual oasis in the wilderness to the great number of troops who used it, and in which many came to know Jesus Christ as their Saviour and Lord. Readers were also posted to Syria and Iraq.

As the menace from the Far East became more threatening, troops in greater numbers were concentrated in India. This fact, while presenting the Association with a new challenge, did not mean the opening up of a new sphere. For many years Readers had been serving in India, and the work was well established, with Headquarters in Agra.

Here, and at Dagshai, there were Soldiers' Homes, at which in normal times annual conventions were held; in the summer at Dagshai, up in the hills, where men went on furlough during the hot weather, and at Christmas at Agra.

Soon after war was declared the troops left Dagshai, but the Home continued to be used for conventions. The same thing happened at Agra, but although the work there ceased for a time, other doors opened at Karachi, where a Reader laboured for six strenuous years, at Bombay, Calcutta and other centres where troops were concentrated in large numbers. Later, when they returned to Agra, the Home was re-opened. Among many letters that were received, expressing appreciation, both of the fellowship and the amenities there enjoyed, was the following from a Lance Corporal:

"May I take this opportunity of expressing my sincere appreciation of the services afforded at the Soldiers' Home. I have attended the Home almost every evening since it came under your management, and have always found it exceptionally clean, and very efficiently run, the food supplied being such as to leave no possible room for complaint. The Rest Room is as comfortable as the best of English homes, and the increasing number of troops ever present there, either on leave or for evening enjoyment, is sufficient evidence of its popularity. In conclusion may I state that this appreciation is expressed, not only on my own behalf, but also on that of many friends who have accompanied me."

The work in Bombay was typical of that in many parts of India and Ceylon. The centre of activity was the Rest Room, supervised by Major Lee Spratt, who for many years watched over the interests of the Association in India as Organising Secretary, in which service he was ably assisted by Mrs Lee Spratt.

On Saturday evenings 15 to 20 Christian servicemen met at the Bombay Rest Room for an hour of prayer, after which they marched with banners displaying the Word of God to their open-air stand, where, for approximately an hour and a half, the Gospel was preached to the crowds of servicemen who gathered to listen. At the close, they returned to the Rest Room, followed by any who were sufficiently interested to desire to hear more, and many times the work of leading men to Christ continued until the early hours of the morning.

It was on one such occasion that a man told a sad story of separation from his wife, and of sin and of degradation. He had been a deserter and while awaiting court martial he again deserted from his unit. He came to Bombay, bent upon further sin, when he was arrested by the words inscribed upon the banners. After a long conversation with Major Lee Spratt he yielded his life to the Lord Jesus Christ.

The following day he gave himself up to the military police and when soon after he was visited in detention barracks, it was evident that already he had commenced to witness for his Lord. He was later court martialled, and letters received from him while serving his sentence told of a bold confession of Christ before his fellow prisoners.

Sunday at the Bombay Rest Room was always a busy day. In the afternoon there was a fellowship meeting for Christians and at the evening meeting, which came to be known as "Tonic Hour", there was an average attendance of 120 men. A Sergeant in the RAF was so remarkably changed after his conversion at one of these meetings that he was accused of being mad, and was sent before his medical officer to have his sanity tested; but a chaplain, whose opinion was sought, cleared the situation for him by affirming that conversion to Christ was a sufficient explanation for the transformation which had taken place in this man's life and behaviour.

Prior to its occupation by the Japanese, a Reader was engaged at Singapore, where he had the prayerful co-operation of a band of keen Christians who were members of the Association. They were helpful in inviting unconverted men to attend the Gospel services, with the result that numbers came to a saving knowledge of the Truth. One was given a copy of the booklet called *The Reason Why*, reading which he became conscious of the fact that he was a sinner, and sought forgiveness of God. A few days later he was present at the testimony meeting when a Sergeant Major spoke on the exhortation, "Choose ye this day whom ye will serve." With radiant face he afterwards told the Reader, "I have made my choice; I am on the Lord's side."

Japan's entry into the war closed the work in the Far East, but at the earliest opportunity after her capitulation these lands were re-entered. Soon after the arrival of a Reader in Rangoon, the English Baptist Church was opened again, after being closed for three and a half years.

It was originally opened in 1854, the first English Church to be established in the city, and it was the first to recommence activity after the occupation, during which it had suffered severe damage, and was still without windows or means of lighting. The atmosphere created by these conditions at 3.30 in the afternoon, on a line some 18° from the equator, can be imagined, but it was a time of great rejoicing. Although unable to meet, some members, including two deacons, had remained in the city during those terrible years, and at the re-opening service one of the deacons, under deep emotional stress, gave thanks to God for the opportunity to resume corporate worship in His House.

When the Pastor, who was a chaplain, was posted to another area, he handed the charge of the work over to the Reader, under whose leadership it continued to flourish. The numbers at the Sunday evening Gospel service grew until as many as 350 were attending, with a regular number of professions of faith in Christ.

A former prisoner of war, who at a previous service had been so drunk and disorderly that he had practically to be carried out, came again, this time to be filled with the "Real Spirit", by whose operation the miracle of regeneration is performed.

This Reader, the only one to serve with the South East Asia Command, was hailed with joy by other released prisoners of war who were Christians and while in Japanese hands had remained true to the Lord.

Among troops to whom it had not been possible to appoint a Reader, Christian men were bound together as Branches of the Association. They arranged meetings for Bible study, prayer and testimony, which were a means of grace both to themselves and unconverted men in their units. Many lasting friendships resulted from this helpful fellowship, and when, by troop movements, men were scattered and for reasons of security were unable to communicate with each other, contact was maintained through the magazine *Ready*, several pages of each issue being devoted to letters received at Headquarters from

Members in all parts of the world.

The use of Branch Secretaries was one of the most valuable lessons which the new Association had learnt and inherited from SACA. Prior to the amalgamation there had been only five SACA Missioners in the United Kingdom, and therefore much depended on the quality of leadership by Branch Secretaries in maintaining the work in Garrisons and Stations. The challenge of this Christian responsibility brought to light latent leadership qualities which developed during the ensuing war years. A number of these men rose to high rank during World War II, and afterwards some of them went into full-time Christian service as ordained ministers, evangelists and missionaries.

☆ ☆ ☆ ☆ ☆

THE INVASION OF EUROPE

The final phase of the war in Europe had also involved the Association in renewed activity and a redistribution of some of the Readers. The whole country was in a state of tension, aware that the decisive hour was fast approaching as a stream of army lorries, carrying men and all kinds of craft and equipment, whole and in parts, rolled night and day along the main roads leading to the south coast.

Readers were busy before, during and after the landing in Normandy, some penetrating right through to the German capital. Those who worked among the Invasion Troops concentrated in readiness for D Day, were conscious of a solemn responsibility in the thought that many of these men would hear the Gospel message from their lips for the last time before going into action, the issue of which was known only to God.

The effect of these circumstances upon the men was clearly evident. Keyed up to the highest pitch, some turned to card playing as a cover for their feelings, and a means of focusing thought upon something other than the hazards to which they were so soon to be exposed. Some were hardened in the process, but in others it produced a melting of heart, and after Bible talks individual men sought the Reader's help, as with conscience awakened they felt the need to make their peace with God while yet there was time.

When, after the landing in France, the wounded were brought back, Readers were kept fully occupied visiting them in hospital. Here again, they found countless opportunities for presenting the claims of Christ, many having been made receptive by their experiences on the other side of the Channel. Some had made the great decision while in action, others without understanding all the implications of such an act, and where this was the case, it was the Reader's privilege to lead them into the deeper truths of the Christian life.

Under the leadership of Mr Robert Laidlaw, one of the Field Directors, a team of Readers landed with the troops in Normandy. Of this perilous undertaking Mr Laidlaw later wrote, "The Lord has certainly sent His angel before us, preparing the way ... On the ship He gave us an earnest of blessing to follow. A Reader contacted a young fellow on deck and brought him down to the central cabin we had been given, and together we led him to Christ."

At a transit camp on the other side, a marquee was placed at the Reader's disposal, where men attended his meetings and eagerly accepted the free literature supplied in large quantities by Headquarters. The men were also visited in their tents, and as the capacity of the camp was 3,500 at any one time, a vast number were reached.

One Reader who followed the British Liberation Army all the way from the Normandy beaches to Berlin, was given at the commencement of that fateful journey the promise, "Behold, I send an angel before thee, to keep thee in the way and to bring thee into the place which I have prepared" (Exodus 23:20). It was wonderfully fulfilled. Step by step God guided, protected and prepared

106

the hearts of the men to receive the message. He also prepared for accommodation to be available, for amid the ruins of Berlin a furnished flat of four rooms was provided, and the Lord's blessing attended the work there from the very first night. Eventually a full weekly programme was in operation which included Bible classes, Gospel services and meetings in which British and American Christians united for fellowship.

The military occupation of Berlin brought within the Reader's reach Germans and Russians, among whom he distributed Gospels in their own languages. Russian officers and their wives were more willing to receive copies than soldiers of the rank and file. Germans accepted them with a readiness that was both surprising and encouraging.

Another Reader, who was attached to the 5th Battalion of the King's Regiment, spent a week in Denmark, where two companies of his Battalion were stationed. While there he visited British wounded in hospital, and on the Sunday was invited to conduct a morning service. A Lutheran Pastor offered the use of his church, but as a convenient time could not be arranged it was held in a school, when about 70 men attended. During his stay the Reader was entertained by German civilians, from whom he received a most enthusiastic welcome, which, after the enforced "non-fraternisation" in Germany, was very refreshing.

☆　☆　☆　☆　☆

PEACE

The conclusion of the war induced a deep sense of gratitude in all Members of the Association, as they realised how faithfully God had upheld them through years of testing and opportunity. He had provided a most talented and dedicated team of Readers and Field Directors, many of whom had been exposed to considerable danger and affliction; and yet only one Reader, Mr H Lowe, lost his life through enemy action – and that was at sea, after he had given extensive service in the severe and challenging situations which have already been described.

It is noteworthy that it was during these years when Mr Robert Laidlaw worked for the Association that his well-known evangelistic booklet *The Reason Why* was used even more extensively than it had been during the years between the wars. It became better known, and more widely used by Readers, than any other tract. In 1985 the Council authorised the purchase of 20,000 copies of *The Reason Why* in an attractive modern format, as it was still judged to be so relevant in helping soldiers and airmen to understand the Gospel of Christ and respond to His claims.

World War II had also provided the challenge of expanding the work to include Servicewomen. In 1942 the first Lady Scripture Readers were appointed with War Office permission. Most ATS and WAAF girls had never been away from home before, nor exposed to the rigours and temptations of Service life. The Lady Scripture Readers were in every sense pioneers, and they performed most creditably, the success of their endeavours being attributable to their utter dependence on God, by whose Spirit they were taught and empowered, and to a strong sense of vocation.

The Association looked forward to the post-war years which, in view of the introduction of conscription in peace time, would enlarge the field of work and continue to bring the Readers into contact with all types and conditions of men.

Military authorities were aware of the need to maintain spiritual values at a time when Servicemen could react carelessly after the extreme tension of conflict. The demand for Readers would not reduce, and it was not surprising that the Commander-in-Chief in Delhi invited the Council to send six Readers to brigades in India, to which the Council was delighted to respond.

Time was to reveal that the years of peace would be no less challenging than those of war, and the same Lord who had so graciously provided for the Association in times of conflict, would continue to do so in the post-war era.

☆   ☆   ☆   ☆   ☆

CHAPTER 5

MODERN TIMES – EVENTS AND ISSUES

The Second World War lasted six years, during which relationships within the Army Scripture Readers and the Soldiers' and airmen's Christian Association were cemented. Nevertheless, the title was long and clumsy. One of the earliest decisions therefore that the Council had to make after the war involved the introduction of a new title. This would require God-given wisdom, for it would have to be acceptable to supporters and Readers, so that neither prayer nor financial support nor goodwill were injured. To the supporters the title "Scripture Reader" meant much, whereas "SACA" meant little, but the Members were keenly aware of it.

Brigadier General Biddulph strongly advised the Council to keep "Scripture" in the new title.

"Nowadays", he wrote, "unfortunately the word "Christian" in a title may have little connection with what we mean by that word; whereas the word "Scripture" definitely binds us to an evangelical faith, founded on the Bible, and the Bible alone."

It was a new Council Member, Lieutenant Colonel R W Ewbank, who proposed that the new title should be "The Soldiers' and Airmen's Scripture Readers Association". The Council decided to present this suggestion to all Council Members, Deputation Secretaries and Readers. Only one council member, Lieutenant Colonel Macaulay, and three Readers were not in favour, and their reasons for dissent are not recorded in the Council's minute book. The new title was therefore adopted on 1st June 1950 and concluded the final stage of amalgamation of two biblically-based evangelical societies whose ministries had both been signally blessed of God in their witness to those serving in the Army and Royal Air Force.

Anybody who served in the Armed Forces during the years following World War II witnessed considerable changes in the size, deployment and routine of the Services. Some of these were driven by major external events, others by internal factors. Inevitably, SASRA has had to respond to these issues, and the Council, Readers and Members have had to seek divine wisdom regularly so that the work of the Association could move forward effectively.

The early post-war period witnessed the last days of the British Empire and the emergence of the Commonwealth. This had significant consequences for the Armed Forces, as in some countries the change took place to the accompaniment of violence. Many of the operational deployments of the British Army – and there have been more than 80 at the time of writing since 1945 – have been in a counter-insurgency role. Nevertheless, after countries became more stable, the Army was withdrawn. By the end of the 20th century there was no formation of British troops permanently deployed east of Suez. It is not surprising therefore that the Association now has all its Readers deployed in the United Kingdom and with British Forces Germany.

The withdrawal from east of Suez was a major factor in leading to a reduction in the size of the Armed Forces and the cessation of conscription. The conclusion of National service was in many ways regretted by the Association as the opportunities for evangelism in the years up to 1963 were quite exceptional. Soldiers and airmen, many of whom were away from home for the first time for a sustained period, were poorly paid and often penniless within three or four days of the last pay parade.

The Readers and those who ran Soldiers' Homes, who were ever available to offer a free cup of tea and a sandwich, were almost guaranteed a captive audience to hear the Gospel message which followed. It is no exaggeration to say that hundreds of men came to a saving knowledge of Christ during their period of National Service. Those members of the Association who are involved in deputation work will not be surprised if at least one man in his 70s or older does not express his gratitude for the work of SASRA during his National Service.

One of the Readers in 1986, Peter Davey, was attending an evangelists' conference and reported that 13 out of the 17 men with whom he was in close contact during this conference had been born again during their time of conscription, and that in most cases SASRA had been the agency which the Lord had used to bring the claims of Christ to them.

It was during the middle of the post-war period of National Service that the American evangelist, Dr Billy Graham, carried out his first major crusades in London and Glasgow in 1954 and 1955. The Association had 1,400 Servicemen referred to it as a result of these crusades. No less than 1,229 and 1,562 new Members were enrolled in these two years. In 1956 Captain May, the Members Secretary, reported that there were 176 SASRA Branches at home and 64 in overseas stations. He used four lady secretaries to bear his work load. He was a prolific letter writer and always referred to a Scriptural message. The General Secretary of those days, Lieutenant Colonel Gerald Clarke, recalled that after a period of leave as many as 100 letters awaited a reply after being away only a few days. These statistics reinforce the conviction that at the time of the 150th Anniversary of the Association there was not one major British-based evangelical overseas missionary society which did not have someone on the Field who had come to faith in Christ through the ministry of the Association.

It was a token of the graciousness of God that through this crucial period the Association was led by a singularly godly, wise, and talented set of officers. Lieutenant Generals Sir William Dobbie and Sir Arthur Smith, Lieutenant Colonel Gerald Clarke and Captain Sydney May were respectively President, Chairman, General and

Members Secretaries in a team which was unchanged between 1949 and 1964, although the individual period that each served in office was longer. The consistency in policy and stability in leadership that this team gave the Association under the Lord was enduring and remarkable. The individual influence and testimony of these officers will be covered later.

The following table shows the interesting comparison of the run-down of the size of the Army and Royal Air Force since World War II, with the number of Scripture Readers employed and the cost of running the Association.

	1946	1966	1986	2006
Size of the Army	1,626,000	194,000	161,000	100,600
Size of the RAF	648,000	127,000	93,000	46,600
Number of Readers *(Full and Part Time)*	94 and 1 lady	36 and 2 ladies	33 and 2 ladies	19 and 3 ladies
Cost	£32,000	£42,000	£320,000	£826,563

Technology has enabled weapon systems, vehicles and equipment to be introduced which have necessitated the recruitment of highly intelligent men and women into the Armed Forces. Technology has also influenced the way the Association undertakes its business. Whereas a Reader serving between the two world Wars depended on a bicycle to enable him to cover his area, his successors began to be issued after the war with motor cycles, and these have now been replaced by cars. Additionally it has been possible to reduce the size of the Headquarters staff by introducing sophisticated office equipment: firstly, word processors and then computers. All the Area Representatives who undertake the deputation work to enlist the necessary support of the Christian public are linked to an all-informed system. Communications with many of the Readers has improved by these enhancements. The day may well come when the monthly prayer letter may be sent exclusively by Email: some 40 are already sent this way at the time of writing.

Another initiative introduced in recent years has been the production of videos, DVDs and PowerPoint presentations to provide the Area Representatives in particular with contemporary and effective visual aids. The result is lively presentations of the ministry of the Association to a Christian public which is inevitably less well acquainted with military matters than previous generations when so many had experience of World Wars and National Service. The pioneer in this was Neil Innes who was the Area Representative for Scotland. It was due to his imagination and drive that "Building the Bridge", a vivid presentation of the Association's ministry in Scotland, was produced. It included the work of Readers and their wives at the Rest Room for participants at the Edinburgh Tattoo as well as the Readers in their ministries with serving soldiers and airmen, and invaluable supportive contributions from Commanders and Chaplains. This was followed by two more general productions "Serving the Kingdom" and "In Sovereign Service" which also included contributions from Council Members and the respective Presidents, Major General Sir Laurence New and General Lord Dannatt. If this appears extravagant to those of former generations, the Council would assure them that these innovations have increased efficiency and general awareness of the Association's ministry as well as being manifestly consistent with the principles of good stewardship.

The issue of stewardship was also in the forefront of the Council's mind when considering where SASRA Headquarters should be located. Captain W H Dawson, both in his lifetime and in his will, provided most generously for the Army Scripture Readers and for SACA, not least in the provision of Headquarters buildings. 35 Catherine Place in London had proved to be invaluable for housing not only the Headquarters of the Association, but also that of the Officers' Christian Union and the Nurses Christian Fellowship. However as the value of property in London escalated beyond all expectation in the 1970s, the Council, after prayer and wide-ranging consultation, was guided by the Lord to sell the London Headquarters, to rent or lease offices in a provincial town, and to invest the remainder of the substantial profit which would be forthcoming. Thus, in 1974 the Headquarters was moved to 77 High Street in Aldershot. These offices were not ideal, but they met the needs of the Association until the next move was laid upon the Council.

The military town of Aldershot underwent considerable changes in the 1970s and early 1980s. As a result it became evident that the Miss Daniell's Soldiers' Home in Barrack Road was no longer suitably located and few soldiers were using it. Fortunately several members of the SASRA Council were also Trustees of the Miss Daniell's Soldiers' Home, including the General Secretary, Lieutenant Colonel Kenneth Sear. After much prayer, he presented a suggestion to both governing bodies that the Miss Daniell's Soldiers' Home should be relocated somewhere alongside modern barracks, and that the SASRA headquarters should move into the vacated premises in Barrack Road. The Trustees of the Home examined the possibility of erecting a new building in the Hospital Hill area, but this was abandoned because of the prohibitive cost. Fortunately Colonel Sear became aware of the need to replace the organisation which was running the Jackson club in Gibraltar Barracks at Minley, and he made known to the military authorities the willingness of the Miss Daniell's Soldiers' Home to take on that commitment. The most effective work in canteen ministry is now undertaken in either remote garrisons or training establishments, Minley fitted both of these characteristics, and Council Members encouraged Sear to pursue this idea.

He therefore drew up a plan whereby the Miss Daniell's Soldiers' Home should redeploy to Minley and the accommodation in Barrack Road be taken up by SASRA and the Officers' Christian Union. He also proposed that the Association should buy the site of the Home in Barrack Road and the work of the Miss Daniell's Home should be taken over by SASRA. The legal and financial problems involved were formidable; but both governing bodies believed that they were directed by the Lord to pursue this proposal. Eventually, the Home remained the property of Miss Daniell's Soldiers' Homes but the Headquarters of the Association moved into Barrack Road in May 1985. The building was renamed Havelock House, although a canteen and lounge area which continues to be used for meetings still bears the name of Miss Daniell's Soldiers' Home. The portraits of both General Havelock and Miss Daniell hang in appropriate places in the building, which has proved beneficial to both SASRA and OCU (now renamed the Armed Forces Christian Union). All the organisations affected by these changes have cause to be grateful to the Lord for the discernment, patience and stamina with which Colonel Sear masterminded the whole operation.

The Council has cause to praise God for His gracious provision financially year by year. The general effect of inflation, recessions, Government decisions on pensions and some policies emanating from a hard-pressed Ministry of Defence have combined to escalate the cost of running the Association; but the Lord's resources are limitless and there is constant evidence of the truth of Hudson Taylor's aphorism that "God's work done in God's way will never lack His resource". Members of the Council in 1981 will recall a meeting at which the Treasurer forecast a shortfall of not less than £20,000 – a very considerable sum at that time. Council Members and friends prayed fervently. Within two months a gift of £35,000 was received – a totally unexpected legacy from a supporter, who had died in 1952, leaving his estate to his housekeeper during her lifetime. She in turn had recently died, with the result that this substantial sum had become available to SASRA at a time of particular financial need. Colonel Sear judged that the arrival of this gift during his first month as General Secretary was a token of the Lord's assurance that he had called him to the work. A more recent and similar story can be told of a single lady who had acted for years as Local Representative for the

116

Association in Sevenoaks and who left most of her estate to SASRA. She died at such a time that her generous legacy came to the Association at the moment funds were needed to purchase a property for the Area Representative for the South East of England.

The Christian public continues to be most generous in supporting the Association. The Area Representatives between them cover Scotland; Ulster; North of England and North Wales ; the South West of England and South Wales; the Midlands, East Anglia and London North of the Thames; and the South East and London South of the Thames. These men visit churches, chapels and assemblies on invitation, and they also organise rallies at various centres on occasions. Retired Members who are willing to become Local Representatives can play a leading part in planning these events as well as seeking opportunities to open up new areas of support. Members and Supporters often make use of the legislation which enables income tax to be recovered by the Association through the Gift Aid scheme. This enables Her Majesty's Inspector of Revenue and Customs to be the most generous donor, and the Council is anxious to ensure that he is not deprived of this privilege every year! The usefulness of legacies has never been more evident. Additionally the Association is grateful to those Chaplains who have directed donations from collections in Garrison Churches to be sent to SASRA. Occasionally Regiments have made donations in recognition of the valued work of a Reader.

There have been several trends in national and service life which have greatly affected the ministry of Readers. It is appropriate to mention four in particular. The first is the "busyness" of today's servicemen and servicewomen which it is generally acknowledged has exceeded that experienced by their predecessors when not on operations in the immediate post-war years. It has already been shown that both the Army and the Royal Air Force has reduced substantially in size and are due to do so further following the Strategic Defence and Security Review.

Commitments have not reduced in the same proportion to reductions in manpower. This means that more is being undertaken with fewer personnel. Service life is more hectic, everyone appears to be more busy.

Secondly, there is an affluence among military personnel due to much improved terms and conditions of service. Those who served in former years would look with envy today at their successors who wear the Queen's uniform. The proportion of servicemen who own cars today is such that the control of parking in military establishments is a challenge to the leadership. Readers visiting soldiers and airmen in their accommodation and workplaces observe the array of electronic gadgetry of one sort or another which is present. No fair-minded person would wish to see a return to the low rates of pay of former times. But the combination of "busyness" and affluence alone has greatly enhanced the independence of service people, and therefore the sense of dependence on those who can benefit their welfare has reduced substantially. Committed Christians can often travel easily to whatever church, chapel or fellowship happens to suit their taste. The opportunity for the Reader to have regular contact is less frequent than in former times. It is understandable that the most encouraging ministries for Readers are generally undertaken in the more remote garrisons and training establishments.

The third factor relates to single accommodation. Whereas the barrack room which accommodated any number of men or women between four and thirty, was normal in former times, contemporary accommodation for single people is generally based on the one-man room. Under the terms of the Military Salary which was introduced in 1971, accommodation charges are deducted from the serviceman's monthly salary and this has tended to increase a sense of privacy which should only be invaded infrequently and with adequate warning. The authorities in some establishment today are reluctant to give permission for Readers to visit accommodation other than by invitation and, as was always the case, to the same gender as the Reader. Over against this, some Readers testify to the appreciation and welcome expressed by some single service personnel who have been visited in their individual rooms. One Reader recently reported that he was welcomed with the remark; "I am glad to see you. No one else has ever visited me in all the time I have been here!" – A reminder that loneliness, even in military life, can be an issue for some.

The fourth contemporary challenging factor is one which is prevalent in the north western quarter of the globe. It is ignorance of the Gospel. The expansion of the Gospel in the last half century has been in the Far East, Africa south of the Sahara and South America. Many recruits today have never been to church or read a Bible. They are unable to recite the Lord's Prayer or speak with any knowledge of the life and ministry of Jesus of Nazareth. Recruits from Commonwealth countries are often much better informed than those from the United Kingdom. In many training establishments, Readers are involved with Chaplains in distributing New Testaments and Bibles which, together with some highly relevant and attractively produced booklets from the Naval, Military and Air Force Bible Society, are often received gladly. Reports received from Afghanistan reveal that it is by no means unknown for a soldier to be seen reading his New Testament, his Regimental cap badge embossed on the front, before going out on patrol.

☆   ☆   ☆   ☆   ☆

ACTIVITIES

The activities of the Association have adjusted in style to meet the needs of the times. Members of previous generations would be surprised at the presence of wives and families at many of the Association's functions. However, by 1987 no less than 53 per cent of the Army and 61 per cent of the Royal Air Force were married so; it would have been nothing less than irresponsible not to cater for the needs of families.

Photographs of the Easter Conferences in India and in the early post-war years in BAOR (British Army of the Rhine) show few wives present; but those of Stapelage Conferences held near Bielefeld each Easter and Church House Lubbecke show many delighted faces of servicemen, wives and children. Church House Wuppertal proved ideal for the early post-war conferences, but when Neil Innes became the Reader in Bielefeld, he and his wife Barbara realised that it was essential to enable servicemen to bring their families. His research was rewarded by his finding the Stapelage Conference Centre owned by the Lutheran Church. These conferences started by the Inneses in 1975 were continued by Derek and Heather Brooks and then by Ivor and May Sherwood, with the support of other Readers and Members in BAOR. They were the cause of much encouragement to those who attended and there will be many in Heaven who first came to the Saviour at an Easter Conference at Stapelage.

As circumstances in Germany changed, the Wardens and Chaplaincy kindly made it possible to welcome families to Church House Lubbecke. Twice yearly conferences were arranged by Derek and Barbara Yarwood, and this routine has been maintained by the current Readers and their wives, William and Tulsi Wade and Lee and Amanda McDade. It is cause for praise that the House is normally filled to capacity for these conferences.

The challenges which have already been outlined require imaginative initiatives to be taken by Readers to stimulate the interest of today's service personnel. Among these must be mentioned the "Justice and Mercy" presentations by the Readers in Gutersloh, Germany. Some readers will be astonished to discover that these are based on boxing! However the attention of soldiers is clearly arrested. Profitable spiritual conversations invariably follow and there has been a demand for this sort of presentation to be repeated in other garrisons by the Deputy Commanders. Additionally Paul Leonard has initiated a Deployment Support ministry by use of Email to provide encouragement and prayer support for servicemen and servicewomen and their families. The number taking up this imaginative ministry reveals how much it is appreciated.

Readers and Members continue to run and participate in Bible Study Groups and fellowship meetings, sometimes in camps, often in Married Quarters. Former Members will be sorry to have observed that the Blackboard Meeting is now a part of history; but they will rejoice to know that the Scriptures are studied and expounded as enthusiastically as ever.

Our Day is still the most prominent feature in the SASRA calendar. The Central Hall, Westminster, which had been an ideal venue for so many years, was abandoned in 1971. For four years, until the Headquarters moved to Aldershot in 1974, the Metropolitan Tabernacle was used. The Royal Army Chaplains Department then very kindly allowed the Royal Garrison Church to be used until 1985 when the council decided to move Our Day for 1986 to the new King's Centre Church in Aldershot, which had the significant advantages of being close to Havelock House and car parks as well as providing excellent visibility and comfortable seating. However it was not easy for those attending to enjoy refreshments in a suitable area. It was the SASRA administrator, John Tucker, who searched for an alternative venue and, in 1994, Our Day was moved to the High Cross Centre in Camberley, which has proved ideal in what is provided at the Centre itself, car parking and accessibility. It had been customary to have afternoon and evening meetings; the former was slightly more formal, with reports from the General Secretary and Treasurer as well as from several Readers, while the latter in addition to more Readers reports included testimonies from serving men and women to the power of Christ to save and to keep. However following the decision to move the event from May to November in order to place it adjacent to the

Workers' Conference and thereby save expense, it was discovered that many supporters, who may travel some distance for this occasion, preferred one longer meeting and this format has been adopted accordingly. All the items from former times have been retained, the National Anthem is sung as a prayer for our Patron, Her Majesty the Queen, and hymns which carry the warmth of the Gospel in both words and tunes sound forth with joy and enthusiasm. The Association's annual message of loyalty to the Monarch is read out along with her gracious reply, and the Word of God is expounded.

The tradition of running a rest room at the Royal Tournament at Earl's Court prevailed until the Ministry of Defence decided that the event would continue no longer as it was not drawing many non-military people as spectators and its administration required the services of one major unit for five weeks, a luxury which could not be justified. A similar work at the Edinburgh Tattoo, begun by Neil Innes and continued by Major Iain Macdonald, has survived in a somewhat reduced form due to the changed arrangements for accommodation for those participating at the Castle. The rest room is manned by Readers and their wives and volunteers from among the SASRA supporters in the Edinburgh area. A simple canteen service is offered, table games are provided and Christian literature is displayed. The Readers seek to befriend those who make use of this facility and to "gossip the Gospel": contacts are followed up. There have been professions of conversion. The military authorities have often made donations in appreciation of this ministry.

After a lapse of some years the SASRA Keswick House party was restarted in 1983 by Neil Innes, who was, by then, the Area Representative in Scotland, and his successor, Major Iain Macdonald, has continued to lead this party. Unfortunately, the timing of this Convention is better suited to the Association's supporters than its serving Members; but it provides an excellent opportunity to bring the work of SASRA to the attention of the Christian public and to pray for the extension of Christ's

Kingdom in the Armed Services.

Scripture Readers still visit barrack rooms, work areas and guardrooms when permitted by Commanding Officers and Chaplains. In addition to Sunday school work and taking of school assemblies, Readers are regularly invited to participate with or without Chaplains in Character Training periods. Opportunities to lead and to preach at services in military churches have increased in recent years. The Lord continues to provide the open door; the Association believes that He will also provide the open ear and open heart.

☆　☆　☆　☆　☆

THE 150TH ANNIVERSARY CELEBRATIONS

The Council was determined to mark the 150th Anniversary of the formal founding of the Association in an appropriate manner. This was approached prayerfully, and in retrospect it is possible to discern The Lord's gracious leading and placing of key figures at the right place and the right time. It seemed entirely desirable to seek the opportunity to invite the Patron, Her Majesty the Queen, to an event. It was obvious that the timing and location for this must be as convenient as possible for Her Majesty. The Association was signally fortunate to have Major General Sir Laurence New as its President at this time when he was also Lieutenant Governor of the Isle of Man, an appointment which gave him direct access to the Queen's Private Secretary. To the enormous delight of all in the Association it became possible for our Patron to attend a celebratory service in the Guards Chapel on the evening of 25 May 1988.

Leaving Buckingham Palace with the Private Secretary, Lady-in-Waiting and Equerry at a little before 6 pm, Her Majesty arrived at the Guards Chapel to be welcomed by the President and joined all the SASRA Workers in a formal group photograph. She was then led into the

Chapel, by the Chaplain, the Reverend J A Barrie. The service which followed was unforgettable for all who were present. The rousing singing of the National Anthem and three hymns was such that the Major General Commanding the Household Division remarked that he had never heard singing like it in the Guards Chapel. Two Readers, Derek Brooks and Meg Atkinson, gave testimonies to their salvation and ministry as Readers and a leather bound copy of the first edition of "Sovereign Service" was presented to the Queen and now resides in the Royal Library at Windsor. Colonel Ian Dobbie gave an address based on Galatians 6 v 14 which is at Appendix I and emphasised the Lord's Justice, Love, Wisdom and Power demonstrated in the Lord Jesus Christ's saving achievement at the Cross: these truths had been at the heart of the Association's ministry.

The congregation was then directed into the regimental restaurant of Wellington Barracks, where again providentially the Commanding Officer was Lieutenant Colonel Edward Armitstead, who later became a Council Member. Groups of Readers and Area Representatives and their wives had been assembled by Lieutenant Colonel Sear and these were presented to Her Majesty by the President. Many of the brief conversations which occurred provided opportunities for the Queen to be informed further of the Association's ministry. As she approached the last group, in a gesture of great kindness she asked General New if it was possible for her to have another group assembled for her to meet. Colonel Sear was promptly deputed to dash into the crowd in the restaurant to collect eight worthy Members or supporters, who had not expected to be presented, to be so. As she left the restaurant, the President called for three cheers for Her Majesty the Queen and these thundered warmly and joyfully around the room. The encouragement that this event gave to the Association was incalculable.

Smaller, but nevertheless significant celebratory events were also held in several other locations. In Scotland, Neil Innes secured Canongate Church in Edinburgh and Bob

Browning in the West Country held a service at which a Council Member, Major General Morgan Llewellyn, who had only been a Christian three years and who was led to Christ by a junior officer on his staff (who had been a Christian a mere three months!), gave a memorable testimony. The sermon was preached by Revd George Carey, later to become Archbishop. Both events were well attended. Most appropriately, a Royal Artillery officer and Council Member, Lieutenant Colonel Ian Durie (who as a Major General was killed tragically in a road accident a few years later after an impressive contribution as the Commander of all British Artillery in the First Iraq War), arranged a celebratory service at Woolwich. It was impossible not to reflect that this would have thrilled the heart of Sergeant Rudd, had he been able to foresee such an affirmation of the work he had initiated in that garrison at the beginning of the previous century.

CHAPTER 6

MODERN TIMES – PERSONALITIES

PATRONS

The Army Scripture Readers Society had been greatly privileged to receive Royal Patronage from King George V in 1913. He was succeeded by the Duke of Connaught until his death in 1943. The Association was further honoured when King George VI became Patron. Christians had been thoroughly encouraged by the following excerpt from his Christmas Day broadcast to the Empire in 1939:

> "I said to the man who stood at the gate of the year, 'Give me a light that I may tread safely into the unknown.' And he replied, 'Go out into the darkness and put your hand into the hand of God. That shall be to you better than a light and safer than a known way.'"

The King had advocated the habit of daily Bible reading, and this made his patronage even more cherished by the Association.

When the King died in 1952, the new young Queen Elizabeth II graciously agreed to become the new Patron. The Association's magazine *Ready,* in its number published after the coronation, included a photograph of the Moderator of the Church of Scotland, the Very Reverend James Pitt-Watson DD, presenting Her Majesty with a Bible. The caption contained the Moderator's words:

> "Our gracious Queen; to keep your Majesty ever mindful of the Law and Gospel of God as the Rule for the whole life and government of Christian Princes, we present you with this

Book; the most valuable thing this world affords. Here is Wisdom. This is the Royal Law. These are the lively Oracles of God."

☆　☆　☆　☆　☆

PRESIDENTS

In 1947 the veteran and heroic former Governor of Malta GC, Lieutenant General Sir William Dobbie, became President of the Association. Like John Wesley and Major General Sir Henry Havelock, Dobbie was educated at Charterhouse School, and it was while he was there that he became a Christian. His grandfather, Lieutenant Colonel Robert Dobbie had been brought to faith in Christ in India through a Swiss German missionary called Samuel Hebich who only knew about 550 words of English and yet he was used to win this officer for Christ on Genesis 1 v 1-3! Other members of the family and young William Dobbie valued the example set him at home. On the first Sunday of November 1893, while spending a half-term holiday in his mother's house at Blackheath, the New Birth occurred in his life. As he was to say later:

"I realised for the first time, although I had often heard it before, that Jesus Christ, the Son of God, had come down to this earth for the express purpose of laying down His life as the atonement for my sin, in order to deliver me from its penalty and power, so that I might go free. Burdened as I was with the guilt of my sin, I realised that this remedy exactly met my need, and I then and there accepted Jesus Christ as my Saviour, on the grounds that by His death He had settled my debt once for all, and that therefore, I went free. As time passed I entered more and more into the meaning and implications of this wonderful transaction; but from the beginning I rested my hopes on the plain fact that Christ had taken my place and fully satisfied the just claims of a Holy God against me, and that I was able to make no contribution to that perfect work of His, beyond gratefully accepting it and acknowledging it. That was the turning point in my life..."

Joining the army and being commissioned into the Royal Engineers in 1899, William Dobbie bore a faithful testimony to Christ throughout his service. Even a brief acquaintance indicated that he knew God. One of his adjutants was to say that he learnt more from Dobbie's unconscious actions than he would ever know. Throughout his service, Dobbie did all he could to benefit his men spiritually, and had been the cause of great encouragement to Army Scripture Readers and members of SACA. He deeply admired their courage and willingness "to take up the cross daily and to follow Him".

When he died in 1964, his daughter quoted him in *Ready* magazine as saying on one occasion:

> "Vital and uninterrupted contact with our heavenly Father is the most wonderful thing in the world."

To which his daughter added:

> "Through war and danger, fame and success, through bereavement, through blindness and old age, that contact grew ever stronger for him. The flame of faith, lit over 70 years ago, burned brighter until ... it was engulfed in everlasting light."

Dobbie was succeeded as President by Lieutenant General Sir Arthur Smith, who was also Chairman of the Council from 1948 to 1967. His contribution to the Association was massive. Wise in counsel, humble in character, brisk in manner, ever tactful and loyal in his dealings, he was regarded with a judicious blend of awe and affection by the Readers and Members alike. His unfailing courtesy to the wives of Readers was legendary. A memoir published in the OCU magazine *Practical Christianity* after his death in 1977 appears in an appendix at the back of this book.

Although ten years apart in age, it was natural for younger people to compare Generals Dobbie and Smith, both of whom were justly regarded as Christian heroes. Dobbie was physically large and robust and in military

SASRA Headquarters

HQ Staff (left to right):
Mr. J. W. Diaper, Lt. Col. K. W. Sear, Miss Helen Black, Mr. J. G. Tucker

LSR Vera Crofts
Prayer Secretary 1982-1993

Reading 1987

Back Row (left to right): *ASR Ken Crummack, ASR Tom Ronald, ASR Barry Burch.*

3rd Row: *ASR Bob Clayton, ASR Ernest Paddon, ASR David Kay, ASR Mel Moodie, ASR John Holden.*

2nd Row: *ASR Brian Henagulph, ASR Gerald Keys, ASR David Gibson, TSR Courtenay Harris, ASR Bob Hobson, TSR Neil Innes, ASR Alistair Stewart.*

Front Row: *ASR Walter Clarke, LSR Meg Atkinson, Lt. Col. K. W. Sear, Maj. Gen. L. A. W. New, ASR Bill McCully, TSR Bob Browning.*

Northern Ireland Readers 1987
ASR Joe Thompson, ASR Jim Moore, ASR Jim Beggs,
ASR Marshall McCollum, ASR Sinclair Quinn.
Seated: ASR JimWaring.

BAOR Readers 1987
ASR Ivor Sherwood, ASR Derek Brooks, ASR Jim Carty,
ASR Richard McClenaghan.

ASR Bob Hodson in RAF Crew Room in 1986

ASR Mel Moodie at the Edinburgh Tattoo SASRA Recreation Room

SASRA Group at Easter Convention Haus Stapalage

Aerial view of Haus Stapalage

Royal Tournament Rest Room 1987

A new Christian Soldier helps ASR John Holden at the "Coffee Bar".

ASR Derek Yarwood at the Edinburgh Tattoo SASRA Recreation Room

terms the more talented commander. Smith was short, always impeccably turned out, and an exceptionally gifted staff officer. Dobbie had little small talk and, apart from an ability to give a testimony to the faithfulness of God at which he was without peer, was not really a penetrating or arresting speaker. In contrast, smith with a brisk, racy style was a gripping speaker with an ability to use simple, alliterative structures and memorable illustrations which delighted and inspired his hearers. For laymen both of them had an excellent working knowledge of Scripture. Captain May, who knew both of these officers well, rated Dobbie as the better theologian. This is no mean tribute when it is realised that Smith wrote a booklet entitled *100 Days* of Bible Studies on selected subjects and that nearly 200,000 copies were printed. Both Dobbie and Smith were well known for their humility and it could be said that both of them influenced three generations of Christian servicemen. Smith, possibly in consequence of his role in achieving the amalgamation of the Army Scripture Readers and SACA, and his long reign as Chairman of the SASRA Council, had the greater influence within the Association. Both of these officers could be truly described as trophies of God's grace.

The first President from the Royal Air Force was appointed in 1977 when Marshal of the Royal Air Force Sir Neil Cameron kindly accepted the Council's invitation. Cameron had made a profession of faith in Christ as a boy in Scotland through the influence of the Crusader movement, but it was not until the Second World War, when he had a most distinguished career as a pilot and was given a New Testament while in hospital by the OCU travelling secretary, Captain Hartley Holmes, that his faith began to grow. His rise to the Chief of the Air Staff and Chief of the Defence Staff had not been predictable, but the Lord raised him up for a definite purpose. His exceptional responsibilities had not made it easy for him to have regular fellowship among evangelical Christians. Nevertheless he was an enthusiastic President who became increasingly glad to be involved in the affairs of the Association, regularly chairing the afternoon meetings on Our Day. Those who heard the fluency of his extempore praying on the last such occasion he was able to attend could discern a gratitude for the way the Lord had blessed him in his work for the Association. He was made a Knight of the Thistle and raised to the Peerage, and when he died in 1985 the Association mourned the loss of a loyal Christian friend and ally.

Lord Cameron was succeeded as President by Major General Sir Laurence New, who was appointed Lieutenant Governor of the Isle of Man that year. A Manxman by education, General New not only served in the Royal Tank Regiment but became in his generation the Army's most knowledgeable officer on the design of modern tanks. A tour as Defence Attaché in Israel had quickened this interest as it followed the Yom Kippur War in 1973. He was much in demand as a lecturer for his absorbing presentation of the key battle on the Golan Heights. General New was converted as a result of reading John Stott's book *Basic Christianity* in 1964 as he flew back from Gibraltar during a tour as a young staff officer in the Ministry of Defence. The appointment of a President who assumed the office considerably younger than any of his predecessors in the 20th century assured the Association of a reign of influence and continuity. As has been stated already, General New's contribution to the success of the 150th anniversary celebrations was especially significant. Nothing revealed his commitment to the SASRA ministry more than his prayerful messages to the Council before meetings and his annually sending a Christmas card to every worker.

General New retired as President in 1999. His successor, Major General Richard Dannatt, had trusted Christ in his early life, but three events in his late twenties in which he might well have lost his life – a stroke, a tragic operational experience and a traffic accident – were used of God, together with verses on the Lord's discipline in Hebrews 12 from a mature Christian friend, to bring him to a deeper commitment and assurance of faith in Christ. General Dannatt had a brilliant operational record and had been a Council Member for several years before assuming the Presidency. This gave him a good understanding of the workings of the Council, and of virtually every worker as well as a feel for the issues which had to be handled. His rise to Chief of the General Staff gave great pleasure to the Association and to the Army and likewise his subsequent elevation to the House of Lords. All ranks recognised a Chief whose integrity was beyond question and who spoke up for the Service to the point that he was willing to state the unpopular with moral courage and in as constructive a way as possible. SASRA has been exceptionally fortunate to have him in its most senior office. His presiding over meetings on Our Day, and his seeking out Readers and praying openly with them at the Rest Room at the Edinburgh Tattoo and at other locations when his military duties have taken him, have been especially appreciated.

☆ ☆ ☆ ☆ ☆

CHAIRMEN

The Chairman of the SASRA Council is inevitably more involved in the detailed leadership of the Association than the President. Under God, he leads a Council of between 12 and 24 serving and retired Army and RAF officers, works with the Headquarters staff and has considerable influence on policy. He probably knows the Readers and their families better than any other Council Member. Lieutenant General Sir Arthur Smith's wisdom and influence during his 19 years as Chairman have already been covered. He was succeeded in 1967 by Brigadier Alfred Jarrett-Kerr, a Sapper officer with a brilliant record on the design of military bridging. He had been Sir Donald Bailey's military assistant in the design of the famous Bailey Bridge which the Americans reckoned was of such significance that it shortened the length of the war in

Europe by six months. Jarrett-Kerr, who always attributed his successes to answered prayer, took part in the Rhine Crossing, and later became director of the Military Engineering Experimental Establishment. He had an exceptionally quick brain and was shrewd financially. These gifts were of special value to the Association during the period in which the difficult decision to move the Headquarters from London had to be faced. His Chairmanship of the Trustees' of the Miss Daniell's Soldier's Home was also conspicuous for his unselfish willingness to take decisions, and he and his wife will be remembered for their Christian compassion and support, particularly of the Headquarters staff.

Group Captain Alfred Knowles became Chairman in 1981 after no less than 25 years as Vice-Chairman. As a teenager when his father was stationed with a Greenjacket battalion in Tidworth in the 1930s, Alfred Knowles sang in the choir at the Garrison Church. One Sunday, in response to a clear presentation of the Gospel in that church by a retired officer, Alfred Knowles put his trust in Christ. Shortly afterwards he went as an apprentice to RAF Halton. Here he was fortunate to be in a group of young apprentices who were nurtured spiritually by the Chaplain, the Reverend J R Walkey (later Chaplain-in-Chief of the Royal Air Force), and by the Scripture Reader at Halton. He was unusually gifted musically and also technically (he built and flew his own aeroplane). Five out of a particularly close knit group of these apprentices at Halton were later to be commissioned and rise to the rank of Group Captain. Knowles himself was decorated twice and it was observable throughout his service in the RAF that he and his wife were effective and fruitful witnesses. In every posting service personnel seemed to be converted following their contact with the Knowles. Group Captain Knowles' longstanding and wholehearted commitment to SASRA made his appointment as Chairman one that was as respected as it was popular. Although he had commended his successor, Knowles died in office five days before he had intended to resign at the Annual General Meeting, "having fought the good fight, having finished the race and having kept the Faith".

The next Chairman was to be Brigadier Ian Dobbie, grandson of the former President. He has always subscribed to the light-hearted aphorism that "a man cannot take too much trouble in the selection of his grandfather!" – and not least because his grandfather prayed for him every day for the first 25 years of his life. He also drew the first profession of faith out of him as a boy, having used the closing verses of the Sermon on the Mount to lead to his exposing the heresy of justification by works. The crucial conversation concluded with grandfather and grandson, 60 years apart in age, kneeling down beside the latter's bed while the retired General prayed a prayer of commitment to Christ. It is probably more accurate to regard this event as spiritual conception rather than birth; for although the boy trusted Christ that evening as best as he knew how, he had little understanding of repentance or Christ's glorious finished work at the Cross. It was not until he was 22, in a year in which every area of life seemed to go wrong and which brought about deep repentance, that Christ's assuring promise in Hebrew 13 v 5 – "I will never leave you nor forsake you" – brought the entire certainty of forgiveness and New Birth. Like his grandfather and father, Brigadier Dobbie was commissioned into the Royal Engineers. His service brought him into regular contact with Scripture Readers whom he greatly admired and to whom he also felt indebtedness.

☆   ☆   ☆   ☆   ☆

GENERAL SECRETARIES

The appointment of General Secretary in SASRA is a crucial one. He works at the focal point of the Association's organisation and administration. From his office in Havelock House he has contact with the Council, the Ministry of Defence and Senior Chaplains, Readers, Area Representatives, Members and Supporters. The post therefore carries a wide range of accountability and needs a retired officer who will hold the confidence of all these parties. In order that he will be able to deal with Commanding Officers and Wing Commanders Administration with both parties knowing that he has held the same level of responsibility, the Council seeks a retired officer who has held the rank of at least lieutenant Colonel or Wing Commander. It is greatly to the credit of the current incumbent, Squadron Leader Colin Woodland, that he has handled this disadvantage so effectively.

In 1949 Lieutenant Colonel Gerald Clarke accepted the invitation which had been sent to him by Brigadier General Biddulph the previous year to succeed Lieutenant Colonel Macaulay as General Secretary. This was a costly decision as he had already been selected for promotion to Colonel; but he took it all as a call from the Lord and resigned his commission. The acceptance of this call was greatly to the advantage of the Association.

Clarke, like Macaulay, was a Sapper and he had been converted as a Captain at the age of 32. He felt indebted to an aunt who prayed regularly for him and who encouraged him to become a daily Bible reader. After becoming engaged to be married, he became aware that he would be marrying a girl who was not a Christian. Although at that moment he was in no better state, he felt troubled and decisively put his trust in Christ. To his relief, his fiancée, who did not share his new concern to serve Christ, broke off the engagement.

Clarke served with distinction in World War II which began when he held an appointment as a Brigade Major to a special sapper formation, formed to extend the French Maginot Line to the sea. At Dunkirk, by which time he was serving as Intelligence Officer on the staff of 2nd British Corps under Alanbrooke, he recalled being ordered to lead a miscellaneous group to the beaches. As the time came to move into Dunkirk he felt free to testify to both officers and men of the salvation which the Lord offers to all who truly turn to Him. He was then ordered to report to the Embarkation Officer. While he was there, his group were conveyed to *HMS Grafton* and he was left behind. The ship was torpedoed that night in crossing to England and the seven officers in his group were all drowned.

At Normandy, Clarke was CRE of the 53rd Division, and was awarded the DSO for his part in successful assault bridging operations in Holland in the months which followed, prior to being wounded and evacuated back to England.

His time as General Secretary was as fruitful as it was long. His devotion and enthusiasm never flagged during his 22 years in office. He and Captain May, the Members Secretary, made a classic team in the image of a Commanding Officer and his Quartermaster, and together they were held by all members of the Association with affection and respect. Both of these officers were singularly fortunate to be supported by devoted wives, and one of the most valued advances made during their ministry at SASRA Headquarters was in their care and support of the wives and families of the Readers. The award of the OBE to Clarke on his retirement gave great pleasure throughout the Association.

In 1971, Clarke was succeeded by Lieutenant Colonel Tom Dick, who had been a most loyal servant of the Association as Area Representative in the Midlands for nine years. Although he acted as General Secretary for only two years before returning to the Civil Service, his interest in SASRA continued as a Council Member and as a wholehearted supporter who was never absent on Our Day.

In 1973, the Council appointed Mr Graham Stokes as General Secretary. Stokes had served in SASRA Headquarters for some time previously, and had some service background as a Royal Marine. He was physically robust and a most effective speaker when on tour. The fact that he had never been an officer made his task especially difficult, and it was greatly to his credit that he never showed resentment in this respect. One of the greatest challenges which he had to face was the move of SASRA Headquarters from 35 Catherine Place in Westminster to 77 High Street in Aldershot. His prayerful support and interest in SASRA was unwavering until his death in 2010.

When Graham Stokes decided to immigrate to Canada in 1981, he was replaced by Lieutenant Colonel Kenneth Sear. Sear had served in the Royal Army Medical Corps and in the early part of his service had no interest in spiritual matters whatsoever. As a Company Sergeant Major in Hong Kong in the 1950s, he appeared on a British Forces Broadcasting Service programme which took the form of a quiz. He recalled years later that one of the questions which he was required to answer involved his having to state which was the "odd man out" in the sequence Matthew, Mark, Luke and Genesis. So ignorant of Scripture was he at this time he was unable to provide an answer! However his next posting was to Aldershot and it was during this tour that Sear was taken by a colleague to a SASRA meeting and also down to the Miss Daniell's Soldier's Home in Barrack Road. At that time the Home was intensely active, with impecunious National Servicemen visiting almost every night. In the Lady Superintendent, Miss Nicholson, and the Missioner, Mr Andrew Purslow[1] who was also a part-time Scripture Reader, Sear met two Christians of singular godliness. Over a period of time Purslow showed him the Way of Salvation in Scripture and surely prayed for him. Sear responded to the claims of Christ.

It is an understandable fear that submission to Christ will eliminate professional advancement; but Sear's maturity and consistency, which were doubtless partly attributable to Purslow's wise counsel, were evident from his earliest days as a Christian. His performance as a soldier showed that spiritual and professional growth can proceed together. He was appointed Regimental

---

1. Mr Andrew Purslow was the Missioner at the Miss Daniell's Soldiers' Home from 1939 to 1971. His father, Mr Bernard Purslow, filled the same appointment from 1894 to 1936. Thus father and son witnessed to soldiers in Aldershot for 74 years.

Sergeant Major of the Parachute Field Ambulance, was commissioned and returned in due course to that same unit as Adjutant. By the time he was called by a prayerful Council to become General Secretary of SASRA, he had reached the rank of Lieutenant Colonel.

Sear's years in post were wonderfully fruitful. He superintended the move of the Headquarters from 77 High Street to Havelock House, the absorption of the governance of the Miss Daniell's work by the SASRA Council, the establishment of a Miss Daniell's Home at Minley and the 150th Anniversary Celebrations in 1988 as well as maintaining the routine ministry of the Association. His award of the OBE on his retirement was as just an award as many could remember.

Working as he was in his later days in the new Havelock House, on the site of the old Miss Daniell's Soldiers' Home, Kenneth Sear must have regularly thanked the Lord for the faithful ministry of Army Scripture Reader Andrew Purslow 30 years previously; and a romantically minded writer cannot refrain from suggesting that if Sergeant Rudd had been given foreknowledge that a former Sergeant Major would one day be appointed General secretary of The Soldiers' and Airmen's Scripture Readers Association, it would have warmed his heart.

The search for Sear's successor was extensive and it was a relief and a joy when the area Representative for the North of England – Courtenay Harris – in the late 1980s made the acquaintance of a recently converted young Lieutenant Colonel Malcolm Hitchcott. This gifted officer was commanding a Royal Electrical and Mechanical Engineers' Workshop in Liverpool. Although both he and his wife were professionally successful and materially prosperous, they had no inner peace and satisfaction. In the summer of 1984 they were invited to go to Anfield football stadium in Liverpool to hear Dr Billy Graham as part of his Mission England that year. Both the Hitchcotts were churchgoers but had no knowledge of the need for the New Birth, and accepted the invitation out of curiosity. Hitchcott was to recall how the address stripped away all his self-righteousness and left him realising that he was a sinner who could not atone for his sin. As the address came to a climax, Billy Graham quoted the prophet Jeremiah; "The harvest is past and the summer is ended and we are not saved." Hitchcott described himself as "poleaxed", but was unable to move when the appeal was made. He struggled until he and his wife decided to return for the last night of the Mission. Both of them went forward to openly commit their lives to Christ. They soon sensed a call of the Lord to leave the Army. His decision to train at Emmanuel Bible College at Birkenhead to obtain a Diploma in Theological and Pastoral Studies and his call to become General Secretary of SASRA at the conclusion of the course seem to have arrived simultaneously.

On moving into his post in 1992, Hitchcott made an immediate impression of being a high grade administrator as well as having obvious technical acumen. These were of the greatest benefit to SASRA as the ever-increasing burden of Government legislation began to impose itself on the charitable world and the need for greater use of Information Technology became apparent to increase efficiency. Hitchcott was also financially astute and identified a well-qualified retired Civil Servant, Laurence Woodcock to act as Finance Secretary. Woodcock, in turn, introduced a retired banker as his replacement on retirement. SASRA buildings and literature were well maintained and he also kept a prudent grip on the Workers' Pension Scheme at a time when the world of pensions was going through change and upheaval. He and his wife were diligent visitors, and most Readers got the benefit and encouragement of an annual visit. He had made considerable material sacrifices to undertake Christian ministry and the award of the MBE at the conclusion of his tenure of service gave pleasure to the whole SASRA family.

When, after 12 years of conscientious and godly service, Lieutenant Colonel Malcolm Hitchcott decided to retire, the Council appeared to be in serious difficulty as his successor did not emerge quickly. Time seemed to pass quickly, there was no response to advertisements and the date of retirement appeared to be approaching with increasing rapidity. The Chairman personally wrote to several officers whom he judged to be well qualified spiritually and practically: all of them refused his advances. It was at this moment of need that a singularly godly letter arrived from Squadron Leader Colin Woodland; it included the comment that as he read the job description the only area in which he believed that he was lacking was that of not having reached the desired rank of Wing Commander. The godliness of this letter, manifestly written after prayer, and the interviews which followed assured the Council that the Lord's man and his wife had been graciously provided.

Woodland had entered the Royal Air Force as an Aircraft Apprentice at RAF Halton in 1960, qualified as an Instrument Fitter General and was posted to RAF Ballykelly. It was here, following an invitation to a Gospel meeting at the Sandes Airmen's Home, that he trusted Christ as his Saviour. The ministry of the staff at this Home and that of ASR Billy Hall enabled him to grow assuredly in the Christian life. His next posting was to Singapore, where again the Sandes Home and the ministries of ASR Bob Hodson and Bob White launched Woodland into active Christian Service. It was during this tour that he met his wife, Sharon, who was the daughter of an American Missionary, the Dean of the Singapore Bible College. In the years that followed, Woodland grew steadily in his faith and prospered professionally, being commissioned in 1976. As one reviews his Service career and the opportunities in Christian service which he and his wife were able to take up, it is easy to discern how both of them were being prepared for him to become the General Secretary of SASRA on his retirement from the Royal Air Force in 2003.

☆   ☆   ☆   ☆   ☆

THE SCRIPTURE READERS

It is right and proper that the Scripture Readers themselves are the focus of the memories, attention and prayers of those who support the work of the Association. These men and women and their wives and husbands are in the forefront of the battle daily and are in contact with those whom SASRA seeks to influence for Christ – soldiers, airmen and their families. Many of these men and women have given up lucrative professions gladly to respond to God's call and, like Moses of old, have chosen rather "to suffer affliction with the people of God than enjoy the pleasures of sin for a season, esteeming the reproach of Christ greater wealth than the treasures of Egypt." (Heb 11 v 25-26).

It is understandable that many ask what qualities of character and abilities are necessary to make an effective Scripture Reader.

First, the candidate must be a man or woman of God. He or she must be born again of His Spirit. He must be saved himself if he is to be used of God to win others for his Divine Master. He must have a testimony to the faithfulness of God not only to save him but to keep him, and a Christ-like character must be evident in his life. He must be prayerful and have a thorough working knowledge of the Bible and he must be under the compulsion of a call from God Himself to undertake this work. If evidence of a Divine call to this service is absent, he may flounder when the going is tough. If he is a married man his family life must be supportive to his calling in every respect. Indeed most of the qualities which the Apostle declares to be mandatory for those who are to hold office in the church must also be so for a Scripture Reader.

As the Scripture Reader is working within the Armed Services it is essential that he has an instinctive sympathy for the profession. He will have to handle operational and ethical questions, some of which may reveal deep-seated personal experience. (One part-time Reader was recently asked by an infantryman to whom around 15 Taliban "kills" were attributed during a tour in Afghanistan, "What have you to say to me about that?") So the Reader must be an ex-Serviceman and it is advantageous if he has reached the Sergeants' Mess; for he will then be able to offer advice to younger men with the benefit of experience, and should have a loyalty and understanding towards both temporal and ecclesiastical authority. Thus he will seek to uphold the best traditions of the Service and follow the Pauline principle of "becoming all things to all men that he may by all means save some". It appears to be the trend that a substantial proportion of recent candidates to become Readers were born again after they left the Service. As they have grown in the Christian life and realised how unready so many of their former colleagues in uniform were to meet the Lord, they have seen the Armed Services as an attractive but needy mission field.

Finally, as SASRA is an interdenominational body, the Scripture Reader must be content to work within the Association's Basis of Belief. It is likely that there will be doctrinal issues in excess of that Basis which he will hold and regard as important; but he will not regard them as being so important that he cannot fulfil his ministry without them.

This catalogue of spiritual gifts and graces is formidable, and it is with deep sense of gratitude to the Lord that Members of the Association acknowledge that He has faithfully provided suitable men and women to fill the noble appointment of being a Scripture Reader.

The training period of Readers has been reviewed in recent years. After he or she has passed the written tests for knowledge of the Bible and its doctrines and been selected by the Council after interviews, it is desirable for the candidate (and preferably his wife) to join the team of Readers and their wives who are running the Rest Room at the Edinburgh Tattoo. In this way both the candidate and his wife get some of the "buzz" of the work and the value of acquaintance of other members of the SASRA team. This will help the new Reader to work out how he applies what is taught when he attends the next phase of the training which is a course in London with the London City Mission. This has been a most profitable development. LCM is only three years older than SASRA and its workers are probably the ones most similar to the SASRA Reader, except that few of them are witnessing in institutional life. The third and final phase of the Reader training is attachments with two Readers before the new Reader is given his first appointment. The whole period of training takes about eight months.

Many Scripture Readers have been unforgettable characters. Such was Mr Harry Stickings. Born within the sound of Bow Bells, Stickings had been a bookie's tick-tack man, a professional boxer and an NCO in the RAF before he came to faith in Christ. He adored the exhilaration of barrack room evangelism and his style in this work was that of a confrontationist. His stories became legendary. The following account of this Cockney evangelist will serve to illustrate that his adventures were often as amusing as they were spiritual.

Stickings (on entering a barrack room crowded with soldiers): "'Allo all you sinners!"

Soldier: "I'm not a sinner."

Stickings: "What's your name?"

Soldier: "Bertie."

Stickings: "In that case my Bible must be wrong then. Romans 3 v 23: 'All 'ave sinned and come short of the glory of God except Bertie!!!'"

Behind this warm, wholehearted and robust servant of God was a prayerful spirit, and he was used regularly to win men for Christ.

The Association has been greatly encouraged when several Readers in recent years with long records of effective service have been decorated by Her Majesty the Queen with the MBE.

Gerald McClelland was probably the last Army Scripture Reader to leave India. He was born in Ulster and served in the Royal Artillery. McClelland served as a

Reader in London, Berlin, Bordon, Dovercourt, Singapore, Germany, Cyprus and Colchester. He was the very best type of Ulster Loyalist: simple and guileless in manner, impeccably turned out in uniform or plain clothes, McClelland's prayerfulness and self-discipline were a model for any young Christian serviceman to imitate. He was fortunate to have at his side a wife whose qualities of character matched those of her husband, and together they had a most fruitful ministry.

Frank Crofts came from Bolton in Lancashire. After service in the Royal Army Service Corps, Crofts became a butcher in civilian life. Then the Lord called both him and his wife, Vera, to be Scripture Readers. It is beyond contradiction that whether serving in Singapore, Germany, Catterick, London or Aldershot they were indefatigable in their service for Christ. It is doubtful if any man or woman in the ranks of SASRA could have worked harder than this couple, and their influence was prolific. The years of selfless labour (with holidays often disregarded) eventually took their toll, for Crofts was struck down with cancer when he and Vera were acting as Missioners at the Miss Daniell's Soldier's Home. It was an inspiration to visit him in hospital, and when he followed Gerald McClelland to Buckingham Palace a few weeks before he died, it seemed singularly appropriate that he should stand before his earthly Sovereign prior to appearing before his Heavenly Sovereign. As Her Majesty pinned the MBE upon Frank Croft's chest she graciously asked him for what he had been awarded this accolade. He quietly replied: "Preaching Christ to your soldiers, Ma'am."

His funeral occurred the following month in a full Garrison Church in Aldershot, the congregation including, the Venerable W F Johnston, the Chaplain General, who had driven directly from an engagement in North Wales to attend. The coffin was carried by a team of Readers and Senior Non-Commissioned Officers, of whom all of the latter had been brought to faith in Christ by Frank Crofts. To the joy of the Association, his wife Vera continued work as a part-time Lady Scripture Reader and also produced the monthly prayer letter. Many regarded her as an even better speaker than her husband! Their ministry was as inspiring as it was long.

Among a team of Readers who were especially valued in the years approaching the 150th Anniversary and who were greatly valued, special mention should be made of Ted Frampton and his wife Lily, whose steadfast, godly living after the loss of their only child Malcolm, a boy of exceptional spiritual maturity and godliness, during their tour in Singapore was an impressive testimony to the power of Christ to keep believers through tragedy and bereavement. Long after their retirement, their continued presence at SASRA rallies and other activities, often as speakers, gave them an unfinished ministry, and their prayer support was greatly appreciated. The same could be said of the Kirks, who like the Stickings, retired to Edinburgh. The Kirks will always be remembered for a remarkable ministry among Ghurkhas during a tour in Tidworth in the early 1960s. About 20 of these soldiers came to a clear faith in Christ. The sight of these men, impeccably dressed in Regimental No2 Dress and with virtually no knowledge of English, standing up as a body of young believers to testify to their new found faith in Christ will not be forgotten by those who were present in the Central Hall, Westminster on Our Day 1963. It can be affirmed with confidence that many of them stood firm in their faith in the years that followed their demobilisation in their testing homeland of Nepal. They were "kept by the power of God through faith unto salvation." (1Peter 1 v 5).

Among recent Readers to receive public recognition have been Meg Atkinson and Bill Woolfall. It is especially satisfying to record that in both cases the recommendations for their MBEs were initiated by the Commanding Officers of the units to which most of their ministry was committed. This reveals the depth of appreciation for the quality of ministry these units have received. Meg has served as a Reader in Wiltshire and Gloucestershire with both the Army and RAF for over

Scripture Readers in November 2012

Back Row (left to right): *David Murray, William Wade, Gary Sinnamon, Lee Philipson, Tiaan de Klerk, Roddy Macleod, Nick Wilson, Lee McDade*

Front Row: *Ken Surgenor, Bob Elliott, Mark Reynolds, Sqn Ldr Colin Woodland (General Secretary), Ray Hendricks, Meg Atkinson, Kevin Wadsworth (Superintendent of Jackson Club).*

SASRA Council November 2012

Back Row: *Maj Philip Shannon, Maj George Ferguson, Maj Jonathan Rendall, Flt Lt Jonathan Greenald, Maj Philip Bray, Capt Edwin Frazer, Maj William Wells, Lt Col John Allen, Lt Col Charles Kirke*

Front Row: *Lt Amy Mcleod, Col Robby Hall, Gp Capt Mark Bunting, Brig Ian Dobbie (Chairman), General the Lord Dannatt (President), Sqn Ldr Colin Woodland (General Secretary), Sqn Ldr Paddy Gallaugher, Colonel Chris Rider, Col John Lewis.*

three decades and her imaginative means of engaging service personnel with the Gospel has been much admired. Her annual participation in the Nijmegen marches, when she has taken the opportunity to "gossip the Gospel" with so many, is an illustration of her spirit and initiative. No report from Meg Atkinson on Our Day or when she is on deputation could ever be described as dull; both her godliness and humour are always evident.

Bill Woolfall and his wife Pat superintended the Jackson Club of the Miss Daniell's Soldier's Home work at Minley, to the north west of Aldershot, where Bill was also a full time Reader with conspicuous success. Bill had been a Master Chef in the Army Catering Corps during his military service and he and Pat knew how to provide attractive food for soldiers. It is doubtful if any other Christian military organisation ran a centre which was so well attended as the Jackson Club during the Woolfalls' tenure. The open Christian ethos of the club was revealed in literature on the canteen tables and the posters on the walls. Officers, for whom a room was provided for their mid-morning coffee break, might easily have passed a flip-chart bearing the stark test; "Prepare to meet thy God"! One of the most recognised effects of this ministry was its impact on the morale of young apprentices and recruits, who often find the culture shock of military service daunting and unsettling. The squadron commander of the apprentice squadron at Minley wrote to Bill informing him that he attributed the reduction in recruit wastage during apprentice training from 34 to 18 per cent to the homely and caring ministry of the Jackson Club. At a passing-out parade, the father of a recruit who was graduating stated that his son would probably not have completed his training had he not had the understanding and encouraging support of the Woolfalls.

The SASRA Council holds one of its quarterly meetings at the Club every year. This has the benefit of the Council Members and the Missioner meeting at the location where the ministry takes place, and also assures the Regimental Headquarters that the Council is taking a keen interest.

Occasionally the Commanding Officer joins the Council at the tea-break with his RSM. It was at such an occasion that the latter admitted to how significant the Jackson Club had been during his training 20 years previously. The current Missioner, Kevin Wadswoth, like his predecessor is a full-time Scripture Reader and is aware that this, like all SASRA ministry, needs to be undergirded with prayer. The working day begins with the gathering of his staff around him for this essential activity.

Public recognition of a different sort has also been received by other Readers. In the case of Derek Brooks this was a Commander-in-Chief BAOR's Commendation for his outstanding ministry in that theatre, where he was described by a senior chaplain as "a statesman among Readers". He had an influence way beyond Bielefeld where he was located. Apart from his superb leadership of the Stapelage Easter Weekend Conferences, his example and teaching caused individual service personnel to travel miles to attend his Sunday afternoon fellowship meetings. Alistair Stewart received an Air Officer Commanding's Commendation for his extended period of service, chiefly among RAF personnel in the Lincolnshire area, where a similarly gifted and gracious replacement is still greatly needed. General Officer Commanding's Commendations have also been awarded to two stalwart Scotsmen, Neil Innes (twice) and Mel Moodie – both of whom had significant ministries in England, Germany and north of the Tweed – and to Derek Yarwood, who served so effectively on Salisbury Plain and Germany. No one would have been surprised if the name of Ivor Sherwood, who was the Area representative in the Midlands before becoming a Reader in Germany for 17 years, had been added to that list.

While these awards are only a form of earthly recognition, and the Christian's real reward will be made by the King of Kings Himself, it is encouraging that the SASRA ministry receives such tangible appreciation from time to time. It provides evidence that the relationship between the Authorities and the Association is in good order.

It must remain the fervent and regular prayer of all connected with the Association that the Lord of the harvest, who has faithfully called and prepared men and women to labour as Army and Air Force Scripture Readers will continue to give SASRA seasoned believers who will gladly "hazard their lives for the Lord Jesus Christ".

Although the full-time Reader is able to provide more time and continuity in building up a ministry, the Council is always interested in appointing those who are prepared to work as part-time Readers. While these Readers are not able to work more than one or two evenings a week due to their full-time employment, they often have fruitful ministries. Furthermore, in financial terms they are exceptionally cost-effective as only their expenses are covered from the Association's funds.

Part-time Readership may also prove a useful means of a man testing his call to become a Reader. Several full-time Readers have progressed in this manner in former years. During the part-time years, their vision for the work matured, together with an awareness of the need to develop confident and loyal relationships with Commanding Officers and Chaplains.

Part-time Readership may often appeal to older men who are close to retirement and who may have left the service many years earlier. An example of this occurred in London when Brian Henagulph, who was the Area Representative for the South East of England and a Council Member, took part in a deputation meeting at one of the best known evangelical churches in the capital. The attendance at the meeting was somewhat disappointing and the usefulness of the occasion did not emerge until a few weeks later. Sitting in the congregation was a former Warrant Officer from the Royal Army Ordnance Corps. As he sat listening to the association's representatives, it occurred to him that perhaps no Reader visited Wellington Barracks across the road from the church, and although he was not a young man, perhaps the Lord could use him in this role. He made enquiries and after interviews with the General Secretary and the Senior Chaplain of London

District and the Commanding Officer, Mr Ernest Paddon was appointed as a part-time Reader by the SASRA Council. Although initially he was only permitted to meet soldiers in the NAAFI, after a year this restriction was lifted.

Furthermore, in addition to running a weekly Bible study group, he was regularly invited to take Padre's hours. Most importantly he saw soldiers profess faith in Christ and grow spiritually.

☆　☆　☆　☆　☆

THE MEMBERS

At the time of writing about 200 serving soldiers and airmen are Members of the Association. Members have to be sponsored, ideally by a Scripture Reader, Branch Secretary or chaplain. Alternatively another SASRA Member or the leader of a civilian Church will suffice. In his recommendation for membership, the sponsor states that he has known the serviceman as a person who:

1. Has made a genuine profession of faith.
2. Is showing evidence of the new life in Christ.
3. Has a desire to share his faith with others.

The candidate signs a declaration that he has accepted Jesus Christ as his Saviour and Lord; that he has read the Basis of Belief, and declares that by the grace of God and the power of the Holy Spirit he will endeavour to carry out the Objects of membership which are:

1. To live as a Christian, personally committed to Christ (1 Cor 6 v 19-20 and Rom 6 v 13).
2. To be known as a Christian by open confession of Christ (Matt 5 v 16 and 10 v 32-33).
3. To make practical contribution to fellowship by regular prayer and Bible study and by united witness in barracks, as a priority commitment (Heb 10 v 24-25).

4. To demonstrate spiritual concern for others by showing them how to become Christians (Mark 16 v 15 and Rom 10 v 13-14).

The candidate is also required to provide a testimony of his or her salvation in writing.

The Basis of Belief, which is stated in full at Appendix III, is similar to those adopted by many other evangelical interdenominational societies. Whereas all officials of the Association are required to sign their complete agreement with the Basis of Belief prior to being appointed, Members are merely required to sign saying that they have read it. This distinction is made in order to avoid treating anyone who is young in their faith dishonestly. The language is inevitably rather technical and some statements could appear overwhelming to a young believer.

The Basis of Belief has been helpful in achieving unity among all involved in the ministry of the Association. Many will hold dear other beliefs not covered in the Basis, but when working in SASRA, every attempt is made to work within it. This has the merit of protecting all from what has been described as "Jesus plus" and "Jesus minus" theologies, that is avoiding distorted versions of the Gospel which exceed or reduce what God's Word proclaims and promises. This policy also has the virtue, in the words of one senior Chaplain, of enabling others to know "where SASRA is coming from".

A comparison of photographs of Members' events taken today and those during the Second World War or National Service would probably reveal that the average age of those attending is higher than hitherto. The presence of those from Commonwealth countries is also evident. In the 1980s the proportion of Members who had reached the Sergeants Mess had risen. This was noticeable at an Easter Stapelage Convention which was visited on the Sunday afternoon by the Commander 1st British Corps and his wife. During the course of the tea which followed the afternoon service, several Warrant Officers and Senior Non-commissioned Officers and their wives were introduced to them, and it was obvious that a number of them were men of distinction and achievement. One had just returned from representing Great Britain in the Olympic Games, another had been awarded the first of two Queen's Gallantry Medals during operational tours in Ulster and another had commanded a Close Observation Platoon there. Although these are secular achievements, they are mentioned as they reveal mature Christian men acting positively and taking responsibility in their professional appointments. These and others have taken seriously the teaching of the Lord Jesus in the Sermon on the Mount about being "the salt of the earth".

The opportunities to witness which are available to SASRA Members are innumerable. Apart from the considerable challenge of living Christ-like lives in front of their professional colleagues continuously, support to Chaplains, use of their homes and regularly inviting colleagues "to taste and see that the Lord is good" provide members with ample opportunity to work and to witness for Christ. One of the most dramatic and exciting opportunities occurred during the Falkland Islands conflict. A SASRA Member who was a Staff Sergeant in the Royal Electrical and Mechanical Engineers attached to 29 Commando regiment Royal Artillery was ordered to see the Ship's Officer in his cabin. This officer, knowing that Staff Sergeant Wren was a Christian, supported his suggestion that as there was no Chaplain available to take a service the following Sunday, he should do so. Many of the ship's company and the Army contingent would be there. Staff Wren had only been a Christian three years and was indebted to Army Scripture Reader Frank Crofts and WOII Horder who had both helped him at Bordon while he was on a course there. The only occasion on which he had ever spoken for Christ in public previously was in giving a testimony of how he had come to know Him. The thought of this new assignment must have driven him to his knees; but he need not have feared, for the Lord stood by him that Sunday – and to good effect. He was able to speak of "the mediator of the New

Covenant and the Blood of sprinkling" (Heb 12 v 24). The officer thanked him afterwards and asked him to spend time in the Chaplain's cabin for several hours each day as there would be men who would want to talk and pray with him as they approached the operational area.

SASRA Members live among servicemen and servicewomen who are materially more prosperous than ever before: but the needs are the same. The human heart is sinful and mankind, though made in the image of God, is an image defaced by sin. The need for salvation has not changed, although the means of presenting Christ's Gospel may do so. Today's service personnel are used to receiving instruction accompanied by sophisticated training aids, and they are probably better educated than their forbears. The sense of need may appear to be harder to establish in the mind, but the Holy Spirit is sovereign and the Holy Scriptures can still be expounded in His power: and when the mustard seed of the Gospel takes root, God will assuredly bring forth the increase.

☆   ☆   ☆   ☆   ☆

THE SUPPORTERS

Those who read this book will already have realised that the work of the Association could not be maintained without the unstinting support and generous giving of the Christian public. Some of the stories of self-sacrifice on the Association's behalf which reach the Headquarters are deeply moving.

One Area Representative met an elderly lady who told him that she had decided to go to bed earlier in winter so that she could reduce her fuel bill, and that this in turn would enable her to give more to SASRA. Another lady aged 91, a former missionary with minimal resources of her own, set out to raise £1,000 for SASRA – and succeeded in doing so.

The deep, enthusiastic interest which supporters show

is especially evident on Our Day and at the regional Rallies. Many supporters are ex-Servicemen and their families, but this is by no means the only background from which these devoted Christian people emerge. Many see the work of the Association as a challenging and exhilarating mission at home and abroad and are delighted to be associated with it. The conscientious way in which they cross-examine representatives of the Association reveals how thoroughly they examine the prayer letter which is issued to no less than 7000 addressees. It is this ministry of prayer, carried out in secret as the Lord Jesus commanded, which will surely be rewarded by Him at the last day with "gold, silver, precious stones" (1 Cor 3 v 12) for it provides the spiritual powerhouse for the work; and it is due to this ministry of prayer that every Reader and Member can be certain that someone has prayed for him or her regularly.

☆   ☆   ☆   ☆   ☆

THE AUTHORITIES

No account of the work of SASRA would be complete without acknowledging the Association's debt of gratitude to the "powers that be" which the Apostle Paul reminds the readers of the Epistle to the Romans "are ordained of God". Over the years officers and chaplains in the Ministry of Defence and in the chain-of-command have been most supportive to the Association. Understandably some are cautious when they meet a Scripture Reader for the first time; but the Ministry of Defence Charter, and hopefully the consistent performance of the Readers at their posts, usually combine to achieve a confident working relationship as time passes.

Commanders are increasingly aware in a permissive age that personal standards of living are not easily achieved unless promoted by a noble philosophy. It is the conviction of the Association that the Gospel of Christ not only provides a noble philosophy but is also the unique means which God has revealed and appointed for men and women to be rescued from the guilt and shame of sin and to be equipped to live in His world in a way which He intended. Accordingly the Association offers its resources.

Chaplains are aware that they cannot achieve their lofty aim of "making and sustaining Christians" in the Armed Services without the wholehearted support of lay Christians. The Association again seeks to assist them in this task.

Although it may therefore seem appropriate to conclude that the Authorities and SASRA have a mutual need for each other, the Association will do well to avoid such presumption. For it works by permission, both divine and human. Its future usefulness will depend on the humble acknowledgement of this fact.

☆ ☆ ☆ ☆ ☆

EPILOGUE

It is 175 years since Scripture Readers were first appointed formally; an event which occurred 22 years after Sergeant Rudd was censured at Woolwich for distributing the Word of God without first obtaining permission. Rudd may not have acted wisely; but like the heroic William Tyndale about 300 years previously, he seems to have realised that "it was impossible to establish the lay people in any truth, except the Scriptures were plainly laid before their eyes..."

The history of SASRA is the unfolding of the Lord's gracious establishment of Tyndale's conviction in the minds and wills of others, in the Army and the Royal Air Force, and of how, in answer to prayer, this ministry "has brought forth fruit in due season". May He ever continue to enable it to do so until the day when every "Blood-bought child of the King" shall rejoice to sing:

"Worthy is the Lamb Who was slain to receive power and wealth and wisdom and strength and glory and praise." *(Rev 5 v 12)*

153

APPENDIX I

SASRA 150ᵀᴴ ANNIVERSARY SERVICE ADDRESS
25 MAY 1988

Heavenly Father, in Your Son Jesus Christ are hidden all the treasures of wisdom and knowledge. Enlighten our minds by Your Holy Spirit, we humbly pray, and grant us that reverence and humility without which no one can understand Your truth. We ask it in the Royal Name of the Lord Jesus. Amen. (After John Calvin)

We are met today on a singularly happy and joyous occasion. This service provides us with the opportunity to recall with gratitude to our Heavenly Father, the work which He has done through the ministry of the Soldiers' and Airmen's Scripture Readers Association and its predecessors for 150 years; as well as humbly pleading for His Sovereign blessing on this work as long as He pleases to preserve and maintain it.

What, I have had to ask myself, is a suitable Biblical text which carries the dynamic of Christ's Gospel which the Association has sought to proclaim, and which should be the mainspring of its ministry in the years ahead?

Is there a verse which captures the ideals of the pioneers? – People like Sgt Rudd who sought to distribute God's Word among his fellows at Woolwich at the start of the last century – General Havelock, the account of whose meetings for the spiritual welfare of his soldiers still warms the heart today – Miss Lucy Deacon who stood at the gates of Wellington Barracks (300 yards or so from where we meet this evening) seeking to follow up those who had been brought to Christ at D L Moody's mission in London in 1883 – W B Harrington whose initiative in establishing Garrison Prayer Rooms in India was so signally blessed – Is there a theme which captures the ideals of these pioneers and their successors, and which should fire the prayers and ministry of those of us who are left to continue the work?

154

It seemed that I could not do better than take those well-known words given to us by the Apostle Paul under the Holy Spirit's inspiration in Galatians 6 v 14:

"Far be it from me to glory except in the Cross of our Lord Jesus Christ, by which the world has been crucified to me, and I to the world."

Well now, why did Paul glory in the Cross of Christ? After all, he must have been tempted to glory in plenty of rivals – his privileged Jewish background; his brilliant intellect and scholarship; his Roman citizenship; and even his spectacular ministry for Christ, Churches in some cases being born and nurtured in the space of a few weeks. Now I am sure that Paul was not a man who would "bite the hand that fed him". He would have been grateful for all these things; but he dared not glory in them when he reflected on the Cross of Christ. Why? Surely it was because he realised that if the Son of God had not died in his place as his substitute and sin bearer, Paul could never have known God, nor would he have ever been able to live as a forgiven man.

We know from other writings that the Apostle well understood something of the wonder of that vicarious sacrifice. I would like to offer four aspects in particular:

First, in the Cross of Christ, Paul saw something of the Justice of God. The God of the Bible would not be just if sin was to go unpunished: yet God in Christ bore the sin of the whole world. And since the day the Saviour died no one can accuse God of condoning evil. Thus the risen Lord Jesus was to say to those two disciples who travelled with Him on the first Easter Day on the road to Emmaus;

> "O foolish men and slow of heart to believe all that the prophets have spoken. Was it not necessary that Christ should suffer these things and then enter His glory? And beginning with Moses and all the prophets, He interpreted to them in all the Scriptures the things concerning Himself." (Luke 24 v 25-26)

But Justice on its own seldom brings total satisfaction to a problem. Witness the formidable lady who was having

155

her portrait painted. She found the artist's work unflattering.

"I will have Justice!" she insisted.

To which the exasperated artist replied somewhat intemperately:

"Madam, what you want isn't Justice – it's Mercy!"

And the Apostle Paul would have realised that as a sinner before a holy righteous God if he only got Justice alone from God, he would have to face Divine judgement. What Paul, like ourselves, needed was not only God's Justice, but also His Mercy or Love.

So secondly, in the Cross, Paul recognised something of the Love of God. He marvelled at the high price that God in His Love was prepared to pay to redeem wilful sinners like ourselves, and he realised, in the words of Dr Isaac Watts' hymn, that that Love was "so amazing, so Divine demanded his life, his soul, his all." And in the words of another hymn that was "A Love that would not let him go".

Thirdly, in the Cross Paul recognised the Wisdom of God. There was only one way in which the Lord could solve His dilemma of having in His Justice to judge sin, and simultaneously in His Love to forgive the repentant sinner. Thus in His Justice, Love and Wisdom, He stepped in the Person of Christ into the world he made to become "a full perfect and sufficient sacrifice, oblation and satisfaction for the sin of the world". The Apostle, who described himself as the chief of sinners, would have marvelled at that wisdom as he saw Isaiah's picture of God fulfilled – "a just God and a Saviour". (Isaiah 45 v 21)

Fourthly in the Cross of Christ, Paul will have assuredly seen God's Power – Power to change the lives of men and women who would turn to Christ in repentance and faith. He had seen some very unlikely candidates saved by the preaching of the Cross during his missionary travels. That is why he wrote to the Church at Corinth as we heard read this evening: "I was resolved to know nothing while I was with you except Jesus Christ and Him crucified". He had seen God honour that message in spite of his having to proclaim it "in weakness and in fear and much trembling".

Now we in our Association thank our Heavenly Father today for the way He has graciously honoured that message for 150 years in our ministry which has continued by kind permission of the military chain of command and chaplains. It is that message, proclaimed in barracks, in the field, in chaplain's hours, Soldier's and Airmen's Homes or wherever, expounded by a Scripture Reader or Member, Bible in hand and with God's Love in his heart that the Lord has honoured. In this way the Holy Spirit has secured a steady trickle of men and women that have come year by year to faith in Christ through the ministry of the Association, which is just one of the Lord's several agents in this sacred work. I know that there are those among us in the Guards' Chapel today who thank God from the bottom of their hearts that He sent a Reader to tell them that Christ died for them, and felt that irresistible call of the crucified and risen Saviour. Like Paul, their glory is Christ's Cross and the world (which Oliver Cromwell described as "anything which cools my love for Christ), that world is crucified to them and they to the world.

They can echo those words of the hymn we just sang:

"Because the sinless Saviour died
My sinful soul is counted free
For God the just is satisfied
To look on Him and pardon me."

Like Christian in John Bunyan's "Pilgrim's Progress" when he came to that empty Cross they have (through the eye of faith), repented of sin and trusted Christ alone for salvation and sensed the burden of guilt and sin loosed from off them. And it is their joy to echo the same word as Christian:

"Blest cross, blest sepulchre! Blest rather be
The Man that there was put to shame for me".

In 1929 an emergency occurred in Palestine and an infantry brigade from Cairo was deployed to deal with the atrocities and riots which were rife. Astonishingly, law and order was restored in just a few days. The Brigade was commanded by a simple Bible-believing Christian who years later was to become President of SASRA. While in Jerusalem he was approached by Christian people who asked him to write a short inscription on the fly-leaf of New Testaments which they would like to give to every soldier in that Brigade.

The Brigadier's office looked out onto the place which that distinguished Christian Sapper General, Charles Gordon, years before believed to be the authentic site of Calvary, the place of a skull, where the Lord of Glory was put to shame. As he picked up his pen that Brigadier will have surely drawn inspiration from that view and this is what he wrote:

"You are stationed at the place where the central event in human history occurred – namely the Crucifixion and Death of the Son of God. You may see the place where this took place and you may read the details in this Book. As you do this you cannot help being interested, but your interest will change into something far deeper when you realise that the event concerns you personally and that it was for your sake that the Son of God died on the Cross here. The realization of this fact cannot but produce a radical change in one's life – and the study of the Book will, under God's guidance, help you to such a realization."

That realization of personal salvation cannot be achieved by man's efforts – not his resolutions nor his religious activity nor his philanthropic endeavours. As Archbishop William Temple once stated paradoxically when speaking on personal redemption:

"All is of God, and the only thing of my very own which I can contribute to my redemption is the very sin from

158

which I need to be redeemed."

It is always a joy and a privilege to witness the very moment when someone enters personally into the privileges of redemption which Christ has won for him. And before I close this evening I would like to relate a personal experience.

About 5 years ago, while serving in the North of England, I was invited by a Regimental Chaplain to preach one Sunday in the Garrison Church. I said I would be honoured to do so providing that the Commanding Officer gave his approval which he was kind enough to do.

After the service a Sergeant Major wanted to speak with me; and it was apparent that although he had been a regular churchgoer for some years, he did not know Christ as his personal Saviour. I recall breathing up a silent prayer that I would be given something to say to help him, and it seemed strangely right to say:

"Sergeant Major, can you think of any reason why you shouldn't invite Christ into your life to be your Saviour?"

With commendable honesty he replied:

"No, it's what I ought to do."

As we sat alone in that Church that morning he bowed his head and prayed a simple prayer inviting Christ into his life. That prayer may have been unsophisticated, but it was real. And in the remaining half-hour I had with him, as the light of the Gospel seemed to flood into his life with joy and understanding, I was reminded of that trick photography by which in a short space of time one sees a rose-bud blossom into full bloom.

Two days later I received a letter from him - one of the most wonderful I have ever received, and I quote from it with his permission. After describing his step of faith as "without doubt the most important thing I have done in my life", he wrote;

"It is comforting to know... that all my feelings of confusion and the various mixed feelings I've had over the years are all part of a perfectly normal sequence of events and I now think of it as part of Christ's preparation for me, to ensure that when I did finally accept Christ it was done with true beliefs and with the certain knowledge that Christ would not reject me.

I now am looking forward to the pleasure and the challenge of getting to know Christ better, and with the knowledge I gain, to becoming a more able and useful member of the Christian family."

Well a few weeks later Sergeant Major Catterall was posted onto the staff of the Oxford University Officer Training Corps, and I put him in touch with a Church in that city where the Rector has a fine Bible-based ministry. He wrote again, saying that in one weekend he "had made more friends than other people here have made in a 3 year tour". He went on to say that the more he and his wife "learnt about Christ and our duty as Christians, the more we are realizing how empty life was before Jesus opened our eyes. The more we learn, the more we realize how little we know, but getting to know Jesus is a labour of love."

In his first year as a Christian, He brought his wife, his sister and his mother to Christ, and he trained to be a counsellor for Dr Billy Graham's Mission England at Ashton Gate, Bristol. He sent a video of one of Dr Graham's addresses to his old father, a retired artisan in the North West of England. His father rang him and said something like this:

"That video was marvellous; the trouble was it cut off just as Billy Graham was about to explain how you become a real Christian. I would love to have known."

And over the phone Sergeant Major Catterall had the joy of bringing his old father to faith in Christ. Thus several members of a family for whom the Saviour died came to trust Him in less than a year.

Surely Dr Wilfred Grenfell, the missionary doctor of Labrador, was not far from the mark, when he said:

"The Christian Life is the only true adventure in the whole world."

Well my time is gone and I must conclude.

As we read the Bible we see surely that in the heart of Man is a vacuum which none but Christ can fill; that in the heart of Man is a thirst which none but Christ can quench, and a hunger which none but He alone can satisfy; because there is a sin and guilt which only He can remove. But in His great work at the Cross he has made that possible – and a needy world of servicemen and servicewomen need to hear this message.

So Christians must refuse to glory in anything but the Cross of our Lord Jesus Christ – the only message whereby we may be brought to peace with God – through his dying in our place so that we should never have to pay the price of sin ourselves – and thus live lives free from it penalty and guilt. And this way of salvation is the same for everyone regardless of his station in life: nothing could be more just than that.

Like Paul we gratefully marvel at the Lord's gracious Justice, Love, Wisdom and Power, displayed and enshrined in Christ's Cross. Surely many of us will agree with the comment of one of Her Majesty's Chaplains that when Christians stand in Heaven and see their Saviour in His most spectacular magnificence, they will see the Cross is not just the central event of history, but also the central event of eternity.

Our ministry in the years ahead may well be costly; but it will surely be honouring to the Lord Jesus and be honoured by Him if, like the Apostle, we can say:

"Far be it from me to glory except in the Cross of our Lord Jesus Christ, by which the world is crucified to me, and I to the world." Amen.

APPENDIX II

(Republished by kind permission of the Officers' Christian Union)

LIEUTENTANT GENERAL SIR ARTHUR SMITH
KCB, KBE, DSO, MC, LLD

"… the simplicity that is in Christ" (2 Cor, 11:3)

It was Lord Hardinge who said of General Havelock, the devoted Christian officer who was to become famous for his part in the relief of Lucknow, that he was "every inch a Christian and every inch a soldier". This description would be equally appropriate of Lt. Gen. Sir Arthur Smith who died on 8th August 1977, leaving behind him an inspiring and abiding influence both as an officer and as a Christian.

Arthur Francis Smith was born on 9th December 1890. His ancestors had been bankers in Nottingham, but his father, Colonel Granville Smith, served with distinction in the Coldstream Guards and brought his family up in Derbyshire. This was a loving Christian home and Arthur Smith could never recall a day when he did not trust Christ, and Christ alone, for salvation. He was always grateful for this and, when in his later years he was asked publicly what was the best age to start presenting Christian truth to children, it is not surprising that he recommended parents "to start at the age of nought!"

His boyhood was a happy and successful one. He had a quick clear mind and was gifted physically. He won the school quarter and half-mile events at athletics, rowed the Eton 1st VIII and was a gifted horseman. He took naturally to soldiering and was commissioned from Sandhurst into his father's regiment in 1910, after being awarded the Sword of Honour. From the earliest years it is evident that his parents' prayers were answered and God's sovereign hand directed his young life.

☆　☆　☆　☆　☆

162

WORLD WAR I AND MARRIAGE

The beginning of Arthur Smith's commissioned service was spent in England and Egypt. Besides maintaining his sporting interests, he ran Bible studies for his soldiers and his soldierly acumen was so obvious that early in World War I he became Adjutant of the 3rd Battalion the Coldstream Guards. It is said that although he spent the latter part of the war on the staff, his heart was really in the trenches. He was mentioned in dispatches five times and was awarded DSO, MC and French Croix de Guerre. (He confided to his family that he dreaded attending the investiture for the foreign decoration as he would have to tolerate being kissed by a Frenchman on both cheeks!)

This war not only brought Arthur Smith honours and awards; it brought him wounds also. No less than three times he had to be carried out of action. The wonderfully faithful way in which the Lord delivered him from worse afflictions and sustained him with promises in Scripture has been the subject of a separate article in a past issue of *Practical Christianity*.

Arthur Smith was to find that the Lord has an amazing way of turning disappointment into victory. While he was recovering from wounds in a nursing home in Park Lane he met Monica Crossley, who was acting as a ward maid. He invited her to his home where for the first time she heard and saw at first hand the power of true Christianity. She was to say, years later, that, like the blind man healed by Christ, at the end of a weekend in that home "whereas I was blind, now I could see".

Arthur Smith and Monica Crossley were married in 1918. Their home was to be the source of lasting happiness not only to their children, but to scores of others who visited it. Only a few years ago a young Guards officer described the Arthur Smiths as the happiest married couple he knew, and in the closing years of their married life together their contemporaries described them as "love-birds"!

Arthur Smith was as strict a disciplinarian in his home as he was professionally, but his children loved both their parents and all of them inherited their Christian faith in due season.

☆　☆　☆　☆　☆

BETWEEN THE WARS

After the Armistice, Arthur Smith was sent to the Staff College as it was felt that he could continue to convalesce and study at the same time. As a student at Camberley he ran a weekly lunchtime Bible study group for his brother officers. Over two decades later, a fellow student, who had by then become a Commander-in-Chief, remarked that he regretted not having attended that Bible study group as it would have taught him principles he would have valued later.

From 1921 to 1924 Arthur Smith was Adjutant at Sandhurst. His briskness and efficiency were legendary and he achieved the high standards that were rightly demanded. It was during this tour that he compiled *100 Days* – a booklet of 100 Bible studies on selected subjects. This was born out of a realisation of a need for a book to help Gentlemen Cadets to understand their Bible. The comments may seem slightly dated or even Prussian to a modern reader, but they are memorable, apposite in various languages and in 1976 new editions were published in America, as well as in Belgium and Turkey. The worldwide use of this booklet over fifty years reveals that it was a labour born and blessed of God, and a remarkable achievement by a layman in his early thirties who had been through an exacting war.

The two decades between the wars were possibly the years in which Arthur Smith's Christian influence was greatest at a personal level. Many who came under his influence at Sandhurst and during the tours which followed as Commandant of the Guards Depot, Commanding Officer of the 2nd Battalion The Coldstream

Guards and Commander 4th Guards Brigade, remained lifelong friends. Throughout his life his loyalty to all with whom he came into contact was outstanding. Widows of brother officers killed in World War I were visited regularly, relations in difficult circumstances were cared for and charities generously supported. He was unusually far-seeing in his practical Christianity for a man of his time. While in command at Caterham he saw the inadequacy of quarters for NCOs and guardsmen, and consequently inspired and oversaw the building of 32 married quarters. They called him "Salvation Arthur" and "Padre Smith"! These nicknames amused him and reflected the respect and affection with which his brother officers and soldiers regarded him. They knew that behind his brisk exterior was a shy man with an intensely kind heart and an unaffected sincere interest in their welfare.

It was during this tour that a member of the garrison church choir asked him for a recommendation to become a missionary. Arthur Smith asked him if "he had a message". It appeared he had not. Years later the two men ran into each other again in Oxford, and the enquirer stated that he now had a true experience of Christ in his life, that he now had a real message, was ordained, and that he used *100 Days* for inspiration for his sermons! The direct question asked years before had set off a chain of events which led to his conversion.

Arthur Smith never sought to hold the centre of the stage. He used to say that he only got promoted because he never had to pass an examination! He knew well that selfish ambition was proscribed by God (Jeremiah 45:5) and abhorred it; but he had honoured God, and now God honoured him (1 Sam.2:30).

☆　☆　☆　☆　☆

WORLD WAR II

From 1938 he held a number of key senior staff appointments over a period of four years. While commanding 4 Guards Brigade, Wavell had been his

Divisional Commander, and when Wavell took over Middle East Command, Arthur Smith was retained as his Chief of Staff. John Connell in his biographies of both Wavell and his successor Auchinleck inform us that Arthur Smith had a deep admiration and affection for both of them. This affection was mutual.

Wavell described Arthur Smith as "a very fine character indeed, a charming personality and an excellent staff officer ... very conscientious and accurate, had a delightful sense of humour, was the very soul of honour and uprightness, organised a staff well and ran an extremely happy show". Arthur Smith modestly informed Connell that he found such praise from a man like Wavell very humbling and added, "I may be permitted to say that I often wondered why he was apparently satisfied with me as Chief of Staff. I really did, for I had no originality and disliked tanks and aeroplanes and all the mechanical things of modern warfare."

His relationship with Auchinleck was no less warm than it had been with his predecessor. His steadiness and loyalty to both Commanders-in-Chief were invaluable throughout the vicissitudes of the Desert Campaign. On two occasions Arthur Smith was offered command of a Corps (once by Churchill himself). It says much of his humility that he declined such an appointment as he had not had experience of commanding a formation in modern war.

The next two years were spent as GOC London District with as many as 250,000 men under command at one time, but in 1944 he was appointed C-in-C Persia and Iraq Command. The CIGS was Alanbrooke and he asked to see Arthur Smith before he left. In his diary that night Alanbrooke wrote: "Finally Arthur Smith to say goodbye before departure for Iraq and Persia Command. There is no doubt that he is a very fine man, entirely selfless and with only one thought – that of serving his country."

In this appointment Arthur Smith had the responsibility of maintaining a supply line through Persia by which over five million tons of war material was delivered to Russia. He had always had exceptional ability in dealing with people, and this gift was to be of paramount importance in maintaining the morale of his troops in a command which appeared to be a military backwater as well as securing wise relationships with tribesmen.

In October 1945 Arthur Smith was moved to India where he filled a series of appointments over the next three years in the period leading up to partition, ending up as Commander of British troops in India and Pakistan after Auchinleck's departure. These years were filled with fearsome problems as power was transferred, and his courtesy and impartiality, which did not always make him popular with politicians, must have been severely examined.

☆　☆　☆　☆　☆

RETIREMENT

When in 1948 Arthur Smith retired from the Army he gave himself unselfishly to numerous Christian charities and missions. He became Chairman of the Management Committee of Dr Barnardo's Homes, of the Officers' Christian Union and the Soldiers' and Airmen's Scripture Readers Association, and of the Africa Inland Mission. He took part in the affairs of the Crusaders' Union, Kingham School, the Evangelical Alliance, and Miss Daniell's Soldiers' Home.

As a speaker he was in regular demand. His style was simple. He sought "clarity not cleverness, utterance not eloquence". He made ample use of alliteration to help his hearers retain his message. There were those who felt he gave the impression of despising scholarship, but this conclusion was not fair. Arthur Smith emphasised the simplicity of the Gospel because he knew so well that many rejected the claims of Jesus Christ, not on intellectual grounds, but because of the moral implications.

In 1953 his only son, serving in the Coldstream Guards, was killed in an accident on holiday. No engagement was cancelled nor any letter of sympathy unanswered, and the funeral reflected the joyful triumph that Geoffrey was "with Christ which is far better" (Phil. 1:23).

At their golden wedding, some years later, he and his wife asked their relations not to give them presents but, if they so wished, to make donations to Christian missions in which they were particularly interested.

Arthur Smith had transparent goodness of heart. He loathed advertisement, exhibitionism or pomposity. He loved simplicity and his crisp sense of humour made him the subject of many amusing anecdotes. Unfortunately some of the best of these are apocryphal, including the occasion when on seeing so much unconventional dress in the desert, he is supposed to have issued the order: "If shorts are worn any shorter, they will be worn no longer"!

In his latter years he found himself having to contend publicly for truth. He detested disputes and could never be written off as a "low church enthusiast", but when attempts were made even by the ecclesiastical hierarchy to pursue courses of action which he believed to be dishonouring to God, he reluctantly felt bound to oppose them. He opposed the 1968 scheme of reconciliation of the Church of England and Methodists because he believed that particular plan was ambiguous and dishonest.

As he entered the evening of life, he sought to pass his responsibilities to younger men. Fortunately he was persuaded in January 1977 to speak at Sandhurst. The occasion was memorable.

"You can tell your father," he remarked to the Commandant's daughter, with a twinkle, "I have heard nothing against him!"

"I only speak publicly once a year now," he began, "and that is in Strageways Prison, Manchester. But it occurred to me that the Gospel which prisoners in Strangeways Prison require, is precisely the same as required by cadets at Sandhurst!" The simplicity, the flair, the challenge and adventure of his Christian experience were still there.

Shortly after that talk one cadet put his trust in Jesus Christ, and it seemed a mark of God's signal blessing that he was destined for Arthur Smith's own regiment – the Coldstream Guards. He was delighted, but insisted that the glory should be God's alone.

It is appropriate that this article should close with an anecdote. The scene is the 1976 Annual Meetings of the Soldiers' and Airmen's Scripture Readers Association. It is traditional that at the evening meeting a number of servicemen in uniform one by one go up to a microphone, state their name and give a brief testimony of how God has blessed them. The chairman at this meeting, as it drew to a close, suggested that General Sir Arthur Smith might like to give a word of testimony. We can imagine, in our mind's eye, the way the General would have limped over to the microphone (for those wounds had left their mark). We can imagine him breathing up a small prayer that he would be given something to say which would honour his Master and be helpful to his hearers. We can imagine a hushed expectancy.

"My name is Smith!" he began (peals of laughter), "and it is my testimony", he added with conviction, "that God saves and God keeps." He sat down. It was so simple and typical of the man who had endeavoured "to please Him who had chosen him to be a soldier" (2 Tim.2:4).

☆ ☆ ☆ ☆ ☆

THE SOLDIERS' AND AIRMEN'S SCRIPTURE READERS ASSOCIATION

**Havelock House, Barrack Road
Aldershot, Hants. GU11 3NP**

OBJECTS

To spread the saving knowledge of Christ among the personnel of HM Forces.

To promote Christian fellowship at home and overseas for men and women of all denominations who are serving in the Army and RAF.

BASIS OF BELIEF

The Supreme Authority and sufficiency of the Holy Scriptures, as originally given in the Old and New Testaments, as being (not merely containing) the Word of God, revealing His will to men; the unity of the Father, the Son and the Holy Spirit in the Godhead; the love of God to the world; man's fall and spiritual death; redemption from sin and wrath to come only through the propitiatory sacrifice of the Lord Jesus Christ; justification by faith; the necessity of the direct work of the Holy Spirit to impart and sustain spiritual life; the essential oneness of all who believe in the Lord Jesus Christ; and the obligation resting upon all those who name His Name, to afford evidence of their discipleship by a life of obedience to His commands.